AF291470

KANDIS WILLIAMS

A LINE

CLARION

KANDIS WILLIAMS

Contents

Curator's Note: There Are Two Sides to Every Line
Ebony L. Haynes

This is the first volume of *Clarion*. Each exhibition at 52 Walker will have an accompanying edition in the series, highlighting and expanding on the show's conceptual theses through newly commissioned texts, interviews, archival materials, and artistic interventions. The series' design is inspired by leather-bound encyclopedias, which speaks to the archival and research-based ethos behind 52 Walker's exhibitions and publications. Although aesthetically consistent, each volume can take a different form in direct response to the work and in collaboration with the artists.

Words such as "conceptual" and "research-based" have become descriptors of 52 Walker—its exhibitions, books, library, and curatorial interests. The gallery presents four exhibitions a year, slowing the traditional gallery structure to a model more aligned with a kunsthalle. Visitors are invited to return to a show over its three-month run to engage in a practice of durational viewing, promoting a critical engagement with the work. The *Clarion* series further conceptually encapsulates the goals of 52 Walker, in contributing to scholarship, serving as an archive, and adapting the material of each volume to the ideas and installations put forward by each artist.

The series name is inspired by one of my most beloved writers and heroes, Octavia E. Butler. Butler was first published in the 1971 Clarion workshop anthology. Formed in 1968, Clarion is an intense science-fiction writing workshop, currently hosted by the University of California, San Diego. Of course, the content of this and every *Clarion* volume is not science fiction—at least not by any traditional definition. For me, *Clarion* represents the unprecedented, the unknown, the uncharted. It maps the morphing of a gallery and an idea, at first floating and fictional, into something real but at the same time fantastical.

In contributing a curator's note, I am channeling another one of my heroes, Julianne Escobedo Shepherd, the former executive editor of *FADER*. Every issue—not unlike many other magazines—touted an editor's note that set the tone for the reader and prescribed a precedent for the content-heavy trip you were about to embark on. I predict, for this series, the tone and focus will shift, slightly, with every exhibition, in line with the range of ideas presented by each artist and my curatorial thesis.

When the gallery first became a real possibility—still mostly a glimmer in my eye—I knew that Kandis Williams had to have the inaugural show. I first met Kandis in 2016 and have included her work in three group exhibitions, prior to presenting her first solo exhibition in New York. She is a director, archivist, writer, collaborator, dramaturg, and researcher. Her interests in issues of race and semiotics and constructed concepts—such as how language, myth, and historiography shape perception—are exciting areas to highlight in a gallery context. Her practice is an important marker for 52 Walker, as both focus on work that is, in my opinion, difficult to categorize, rigorous, thoughtful, and demanding.

The pieces Kandis created for *A Line* move toward a formal dance notation, and throughout the course of the exhibition and the production of this volume, she has continued to ruminate on the concept of "a line": what it is and what it means. Through *Clarion*, Kandis's ongoing contemplation is contextualized and expanded, a reverie frozen at one particular moment in time.

In ten years from now, when people look back at the *Clarion* series and the 52 Walker exhibition history and archive, I hope that together they uncover clear through lines to what, for some, may have not been such obvious connections at the time. Hopefully, readers will look evermore forward to the next ten years of 52 Walker. Until then, question everything.

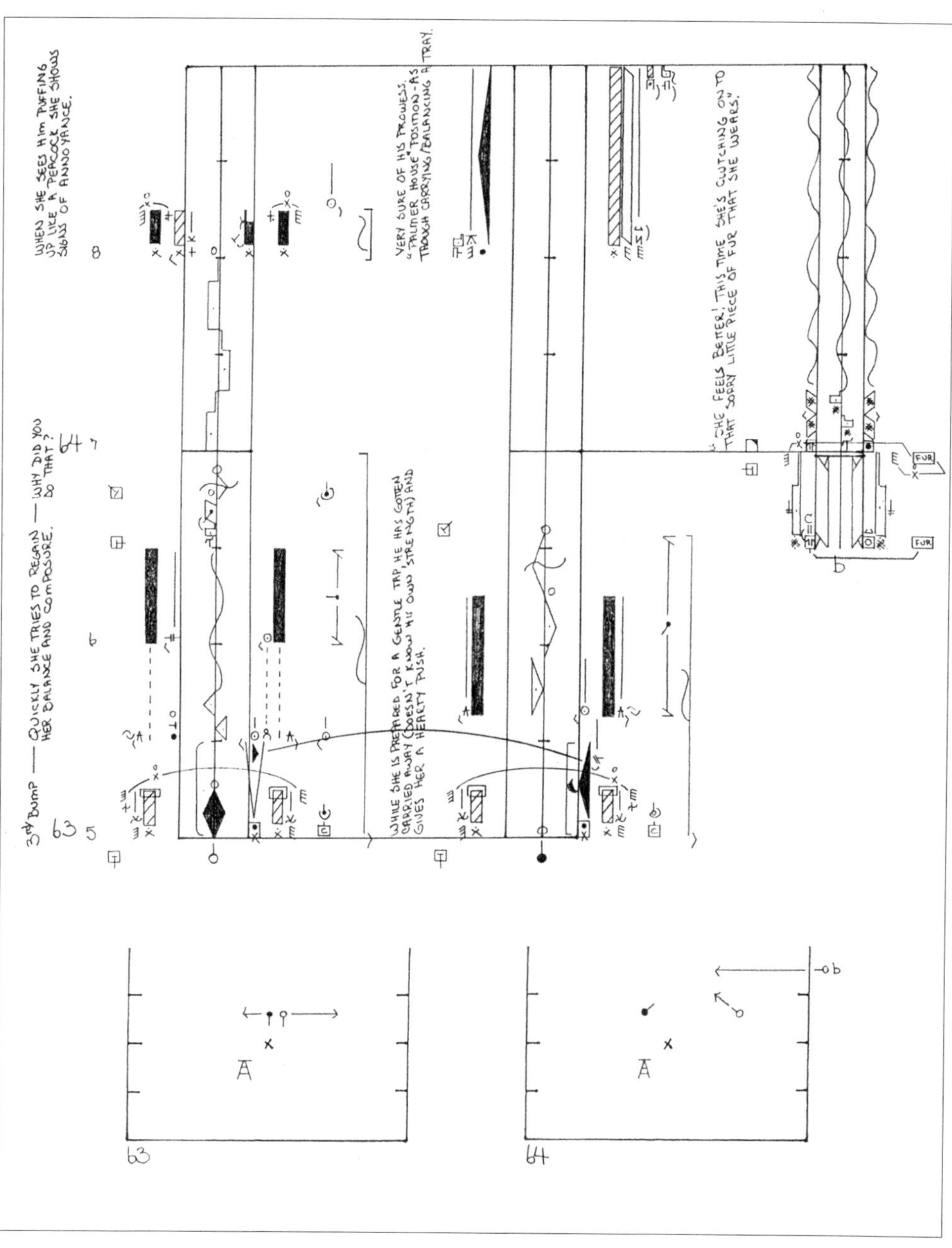

Page from the Labanotation score of
Katherine Dunham's *Barrelhouse Blues*, n.d.

Magical First Equipment
Hannah Black

Dance is the most ephemeral of the arts because the human body is the most ephemeral of media. In the centuries before film and photography, choreography could be preserved only through imitation and apprenticeship—more often, it was lost entirely, surviving only as anecdote. Unlike painting or sculpture, dance had no material existence outside of the body; unlike music, it had no system of notation. Until the invention of Labanotation in the early twentieth century, there was no inscription system available to preserve choreography as an inheritance. In this evanescence, dance as an elite art form sharply contrasted with Indigenous, African, and folk dances, many of which were transmitted across generations via a thick social weave of repetitions.

Kandis Williams's point of departure for the body of work in *A Line* was the practice of dance notation, with its encrustations of domination, exploitation, and stifled images of liberation. As an open abstraction of the living body, notation resembles—in microcosm—the absurdities and infelicities of race, if not its violence (though the toll of dance on dancers' bodies, often disabled relatively early in life by the physical intensity of their labor, evokes plantation logics). Though the lines and grids of notation do not appear in *A Line*, its history illuminates a central concern of Williams's oeuvre: modernism as formally reliant on and consisting of a redoubling of race.

Rudolf Laban began work on Labanotation in 1916 and published the first complete manual in 1928.[1] He used his system to coordinate vast "movement choirs" in Germany and Austria, parades featuring thousands of workers performing choreography based on his observations of their daily labor. Laban envisaged his choreography as making labor more pleasurable because it more closely configured to the worker's instinctive movements. (The idea of work that frees is often associated with fascism, as with the notorious sign over Auschwitz, but early twentieth-century left-wing political movements were also captivated by the promise of work. Critiques of labor as such require the standpoint of the colony and the plantation—Karl Marx draws examples of the refusal of work from Jamaica and Australia.)

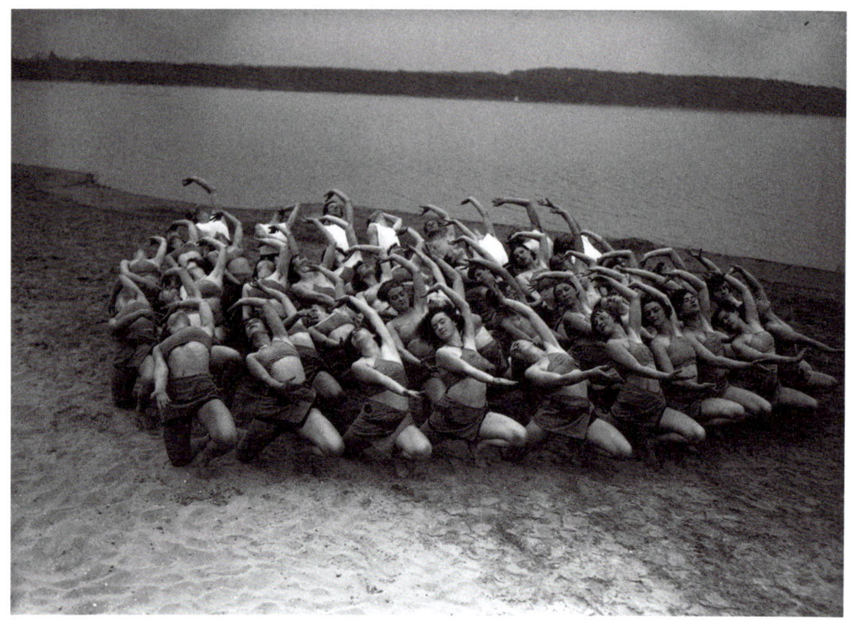

Students at the Laban Dance School performing on
the beach in Wannsee, Germany, 1930

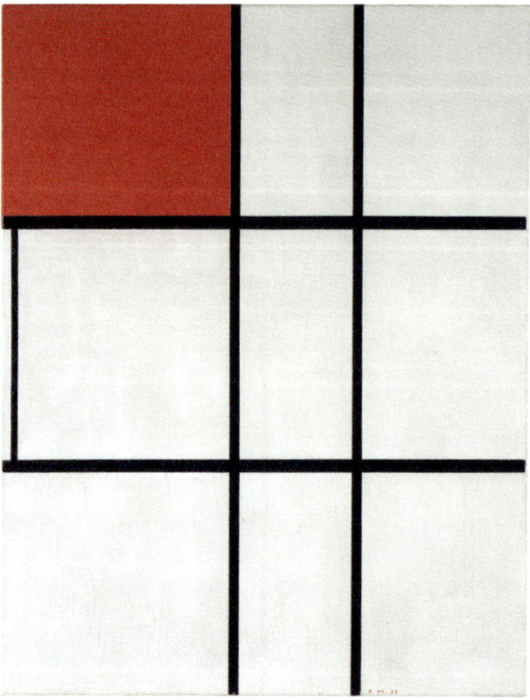

Piet Mondrian, *Composition B (No.II) with Red*, 1935.
Oil on canvas, 46 ¾ × 40 inches | 118.8 × 101.5 cm

The synchronized masses are a politically ambivalent signifier: they are also part of the imaginary of twentieth-century communism and socialism. But Laban had been raised in a military family amid a swirl of nationalist fantasies—his practice converged neatly with fascism's dreams of total social control. From 1933 until he emigrated in 1936, he held the newly created post of Minister of Dance in the Nazi government. Dance claimed for itself a special place in the fascist remaking of German culture. In 1933, the dance critic Fritz Böhme wrote to Joseph Goebbels: "Dance is a race question. There is no international, supra-racial dance form."[2] Laban was in agreement. Böhme felt that dance was uniquely able to "defend racial values and ward off the influx of alien movements and gestures.…It could be effectively employed against instinct-uncertainty and weaknesses, which alien gesticulations create."[3]

Laban's ministry was not a success—he had no talent as a bureaucrat. But after moving to England in 1936, he reconfigured Labanotation for use as a labor-management tool that promised productivity gains. On one occasion, he designed a physical training regimen to help wartime women workers adjust to heavy-lifting jobs customarily performed by men. Laban's regulated and rationalized approach to movement made his work a perfect match for the then nascent industry of management consultancy. His transition from Nazi mass spectacle to English factories follows the arc of history: the symbolic and sentimental brutality of Nazism superseded by the arid neutrality of capitalist technocracy.

Labanotation's inclination toward the commodity was affirmed when an American organization, the Dance Notation Bureau, pioneered its use as a means of copyrighting dance. The system that Laban had originated in order to facilitate a racial purification of movement became a tool for its legal commodification and capture. Just as Laban's fascist innovations found a nationally characteristic home in England through the control and rationalization of labor, in the United States they landed in the mutually constitutive overlap between the rule of commodity and the rule of law.

Like the image of the crowd moving as one, the legacy of Labanotation is more politically multivalent than these examples allow. But its origins amplify the resonance of domination in the act of abstracting physical movement into a system of rectangles and lines. It echoes, though from a different angle, Rosalind Krauss's observations on that modernist ur-form, the grid: "Flattened, geometricized, ordered, it is antinatural, antimimetic, antireal."[4] Discussing Piet Mondrian's linear abstractions, T. J. Clark declares the flight from mimesis impossible. Twentieth-century abstract painting's doomed efforts to rid itself of figuration aim to "have painting be a kind of writing at last, and therefore write a script that none of us has read before…[but n]ature simply will not go away."[5] Akin to the problem of social reproduction in capitalism—for money to be able to go on producing money, not everyone can be cannibalized and discarded—the problem of nature versus the line is that of life surveilled and threatened by dead labor.

On the other hand, modernism is not just the reduction of nature to the abstract line but a dream of immediacy and the reassertion of the senses in the face of the really existing social abstractions of labor and race. As Clark puts it, modernism is possessed by "two great wishes. It wanted its audience to be led toward a recognition of the social reality of the sign (away from the comforts of narrative and illusionism, was the claim); but equally it dreamed of turning the sign back to a bedrock of World/Nature/Sensation/Subjectivity which the to-and-fro of capitalism had all but destroyed."[6]

In dance, the lure of the line was not only present in notation. Classical ballet turned around the fulcrum of a straight spine and emphasized the length of the limbs. Modern dance developed, rather than broke with, this aspect of ballet; ostensible deviations only reinforced the inheritance. Though the choreographer Martha Graham directed her dancers to curl their bodies inward and lie down on the floor, her eponymous technique was still organized around the five basic positions of ballet. In a 1975 video demonstrating Graham's technique, she can be heard in voiceover as three dancers bend over outstretched legs: "This shows the magical first equipment of

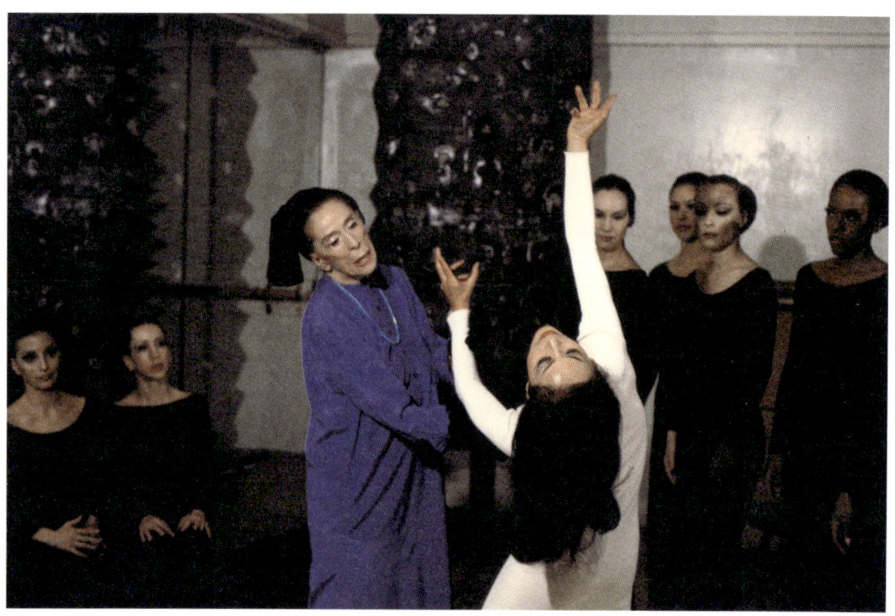

Martha Graham rehearses Takako Asakawa and
dancers in *Heretic*, 1986

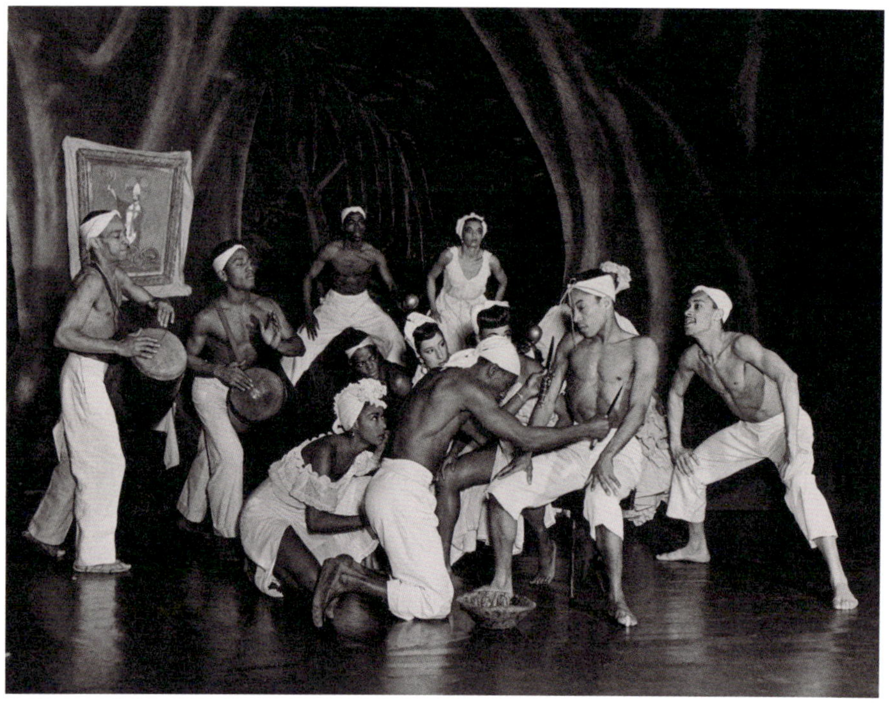

Katherine Dunham's ballet *Shango*, from *A Caribbean Rhapsody*,
at the Royal Court Theatre, London, 1947

a dancer, the lovely straight back and the pliable body."[7] As in other modernisms—painting, literature—the apparent transgression is more homage than iconoclasm. Modernist choreography refines and intensifies the linearity of ballet.

When the grid is given volume by three-dimensional space, it becomes a moral infrastructure. Writing about the photographer Cindy Sherman, Krauss surmises that the vertical is the plane of coherence and beauty, and the horizontal is the plane of base matter, disorganized flesh.[8] This is one of the many claims about modernism synthesized by Kandis Williams in *A Line*—the exhibition is a physical theory of history outlined through a taxonomy of dance. Here, dance is a metonym for the cultural mechanisms through which the body becomes, as the anthropologist Mary Douglas put it, "an image of society."[9]

It was, of course, not only in dance that abstraction's residual fantasy of natural, spontaneous expression was associated with the social fact of blackness. But dance, a matter of the body, could not break with figuration as could other art forms. The line of abstraction took on the guise of racial distinction. Where white dancers were ethereal, black dancers were animalistic; where white dancers were purified by discipline, black dancers were animated by atavistic feeling. Mapped on vertical and horizontal lines, oriented according to imaginary planes, the moving body became an image of race.

Jared Sexton has argued that race is itself a line: "Not coincidentally, the etymological roots of *race* link it to writing—to the scratch, the mark, the line."[10] This line exists insofar as it must be prevented from "going astray." To this end, a system to manage excess social energies, which Sexton calls "the general economy of race[,] endlessly produces . . . *bodies as images*—not images *of* bodies, but rather *living images* of race."[11] This racializing system posits miscegenation/multiracialism as an avant-garde, a boundary at which race is threatened with deconstruction, in order to reinforce the anchoring power of "the black body image."

The avant-garde of dance also allowed the line of race to stray. Alluring and threatening hybrids, infusions of otherworldly energies, ultimately affirmed the black body image as the central truth of race. The modernization of dance explicitly involved the assimilation of the "alien gesticulations" identified by Böhme in his pitch to the Nazi government. "The alien dancing bodies of modern dancers exemplified what modernity could do for you and what it did to you," writes Ramsay Burt. "As the dancer took modernity inside him or herself s/he embodied it through dancing to jungle music and the song of the machine."[12] Josephine Baker, star of the jungle and of the machine, was a trained performer drawing on multiple traditions who became famous for her *danse sauvage* (savage dance). It was hoped and feared that Baker's work would reintroduce the primitive vitality of Africa into European culture, paradoxically making Europe modern through an infusion of prehistory. As with the integration of West African agricultural expertise into American rice cultivation through the appropriated knowledge of supposedly brute slaves, advanced technique was co-opted under the sign of wild nature.

"We have two primitive sources," said Martha Graham in 1930, "dangerous and hard to handle in the arts, but of intense psychic significance— the Indian and the Negro. That these influence us is certain—the Negro with his rhythms of disintegration, the Indian by his intense integration, his sense of ritualistic tribal drama." For Graham, America also represented a paradoxically modern instance of the primitive, a naive movement into open space—the white nation as a form of choreography: "Throughout the country will come the great mass drama that is the American Dance."[13] The degradations of slavery and colonization are reimagined as muses, nourishing supplements to the business of creation. (Despite Graham's kooky fixations, she hired and worked closely with black dancers from the early 1950s onward. Perhaps she looked to these dancers for reassurance that the primitive source was close at hand, but they were not her dupes—black performers such as Mary Hinkson forged their own artistries within Graham's choreography and beyond.)

Black artists turned the fantasy of the primitive to more constructive ends, following a principle of cultural survivals rather than discontinuity with

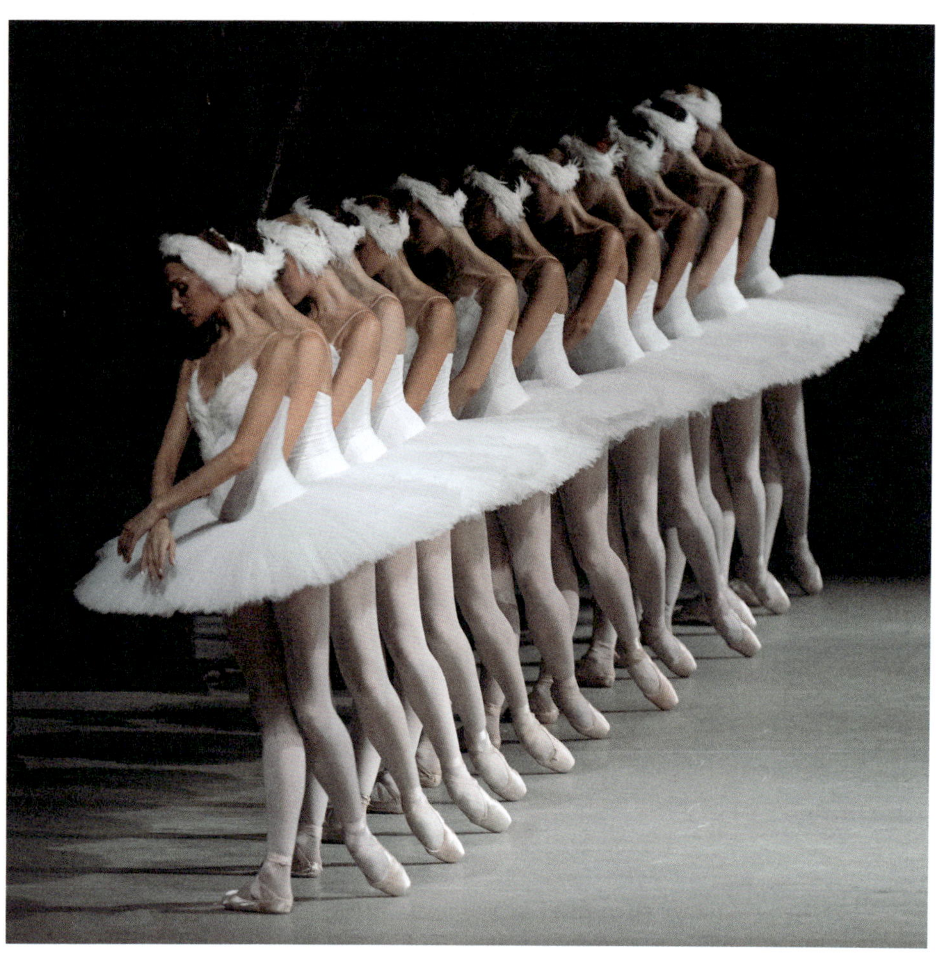

Corps de ballet of the Mariinsky Ballet in
Swan Lake, 2012

the past. The American dance artist Katherine Dunham went to Haiti to learn ritual dances of African origin, synthesized in the impossible conditions of the plantation and further developed in its revolutionary aftermath. Dunham felt this was movement that still retained its social power: the power to maintain life and ritualize conflict. She looked to its forms as antidotes to ambient anti-blackness in the United States. These embodied mechanisms of social integration offered, she thought, communal protection against the perception and imposition of blackness as a state of disintegration. The plantation, more than any other social form, inaugurated modernity—C. L. R. James called the slaves of the Caribbean the first modern proletariat in the world, just as W. E. B. Du Bois named the slave uprising that won the Civil War for the North the first general strike.[14] Blackness is the vanguard of the modern, and Dunham's impulse was quintessentially modernist in its desire to access a prior condition of unmediated, collective experience.

It does not seem merely coincidental that ballet emerged in the same time and place as the capitalist world economy, in fifteenth-century Italian Renaissance courts. *The corps de ballet* (body of the ballet), a somewhat later innovation, is a mass of identical dancers performing identical movements. The corps anticipates the chorus line and the factory line and implies the line of race. After abolition, the encounter between the courtly European formalism of ballet and black vernacular dance produced the distinctive character of American modern dance. This form developed alongside the mutations and canalizations of the plantation that re-created race as a civil and political question. Meanwhile, by the same token, they drove its lethal symbolisms deeper into the terrain of the unconscious. Movement fragmented into the spasm, the symptom, or coagulated into fascist spectacle and corporate management. Yet in the sphere of black social dance, movement continued to signify freedom—not the grand horizons of modernism, nor those of its thwarted correlate, revolution, but an immanent liberation grounded in the vitality of the body. Shared rhythms contained and collectivized feeling. In 1945, Dunham

made the patriotic claim that the jitterbug, originating in Jamaica, "relieves the tension in violent dance very free and unconfined. This freedom in the dance is an indication of freedom in our society."[15] At Paradise Garage in the 1970s and '80s, the long hours of the all-night dance party expanded the time and social space outside the working day. Unlike Laban's mass spectacles or Graham's fidelity to technique, this was movement as the negation of labor.

Without this negation, dance becomes race play—as Graham and Laban openly recognized— if only because the body directly mediates history. Stance, gesture, and gait are cultural and hereditary—freighted with dead generations no less than politics and art. Whenever it is scripted by labor and the commodity, dance is condemned to reinstate the black body image that anchors the teeming, pestilent vessel of race. In the vernacular dances of TikTok and surreal celebrity bodies (zones of production of blackface), the "primitive source" hypertrophies, flattens, spins: on one side, an image of compulsory jouissance; on the other, an image of boundless abjection— faster, faster, until the two images blur, until this blurred entity appears animate. "The reduction of the black body to pure myth or pure virtual image becomes the language that we're stuck in,"[16] says Williams of this hectic stasis. Thus, in her collages, body parts and gestures repeat in eidetic despair—though not without beauty, which is a form of hope. Never entirely captured by grid or line, the force that moves the body also moves the world.

Notes

1 Whitney Elaine Laemmli, "The Choreography of Everyday Life: Rudolf Laban and the Making of Modern Movement" (PhD diss., University of Pennsylvania, 2016), https://repository.upenn .edu/edissertations/1823/. The majority of historical facts about Laban's career in this essay are from this dissertation.

2 Quoted in Lilian Karina and Marion Kant, *Hitler's Dancers: German Modern Dance and the Third Reich*, trans. Jonathan Steinberg (New York: Berghahn Books, 2004), p. 95.

3 Quoted in Laemmli, "The Choreography of Everyday Life," p. 50.

4 Rosalind Krauss, "Grids," *October* 9 (Summer 1979), p. 50.

5 T. J. Clark, *Farewell to an Idea: Episodes from a History of Modernism* (New Haven, CT: Yale University Press, 1999), p. 365.

6 Clark, *Farewell to an Idea*, pp. 9–10.

7 "The Martha Graham Technique," performed by The Martha Graham Dance Company, filmed under the supervision of Martha Graham, assisted by Ross Parkes, 1975, video, https://www .youtube.com/watch?v=FuCbs25LGh0.

8 Rosalind Krauss, *Cindy Sherman 1975–1993* (New York: Rizzoli, 1993).

9 Mary Douglas, *Natural Symbols: Explorations in Cosmology* (London: Routledge, 2003), p. 78.

10 Jared Sexton, *Amalgamation Schemes: Antiblackness and the Critique of Multiracialism* (Minneapolis: University of Minnesota Press, 2008), p. 29.

11 Sexton, *Amalgamation Schemes*, p. 29.

12 Ramsay Burt, *Alien Bodies: Representations of Modernity, "Race" and Nation in Early Modern Dance* (London: Routledge, 1998), p. 165.

13 Quoted in Mark Franko, *Dancing Modernism/ Performing Politics* (Bloomington, IN: Indiana University Press, 1995), p. 64.

14 W. E. B. Du Bois, *Black Reconstruction in America 1860–1880* (New York: The Free Press, 1998). Originally published as *Black Reconstruction* (New York: Harcourt, Brace, 1935).

15 Quoted in Burt, *Alien Bodies*, p. 162.

16 Kandis Williams, in conversation with the author, July 22, 2021.

PLATES

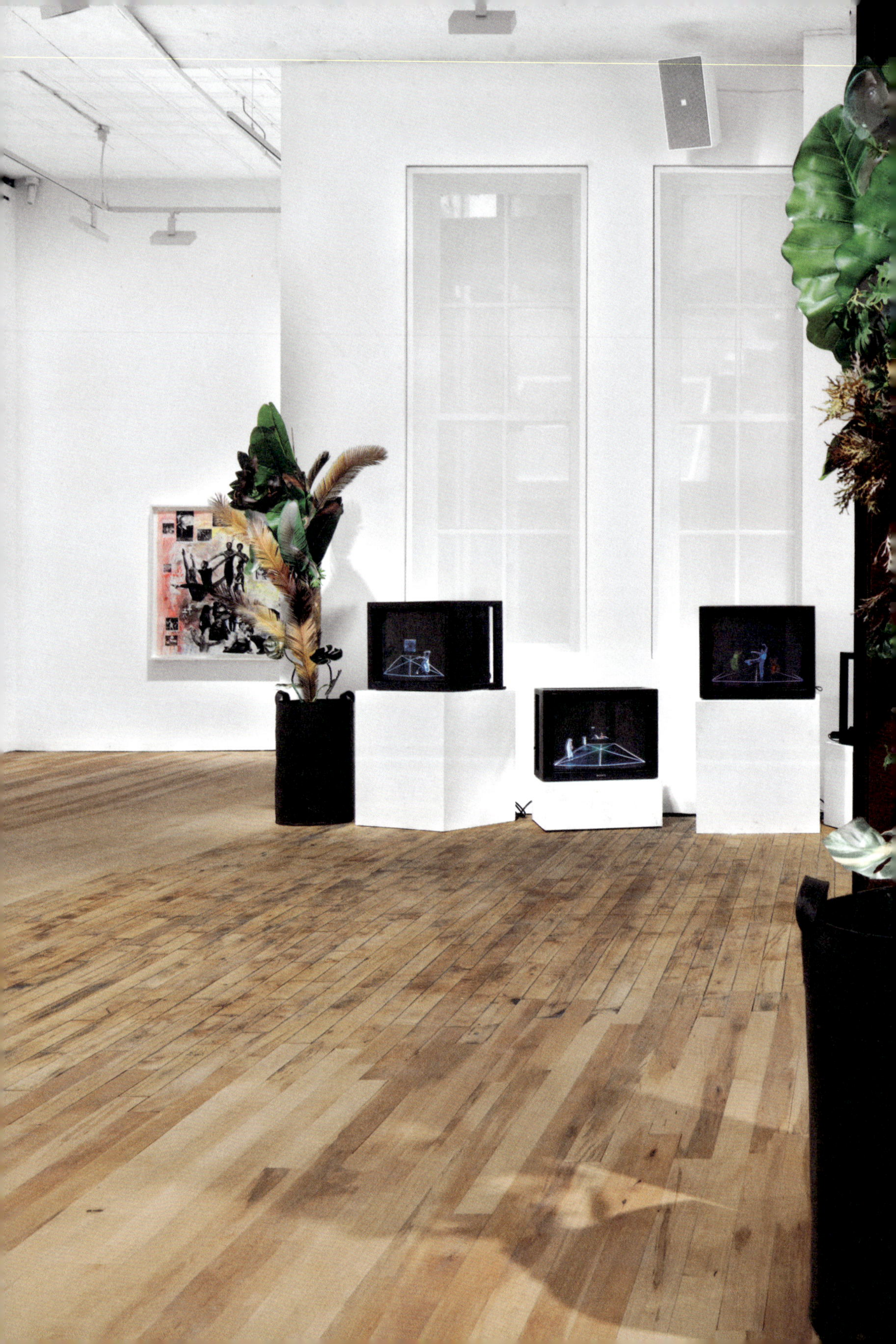

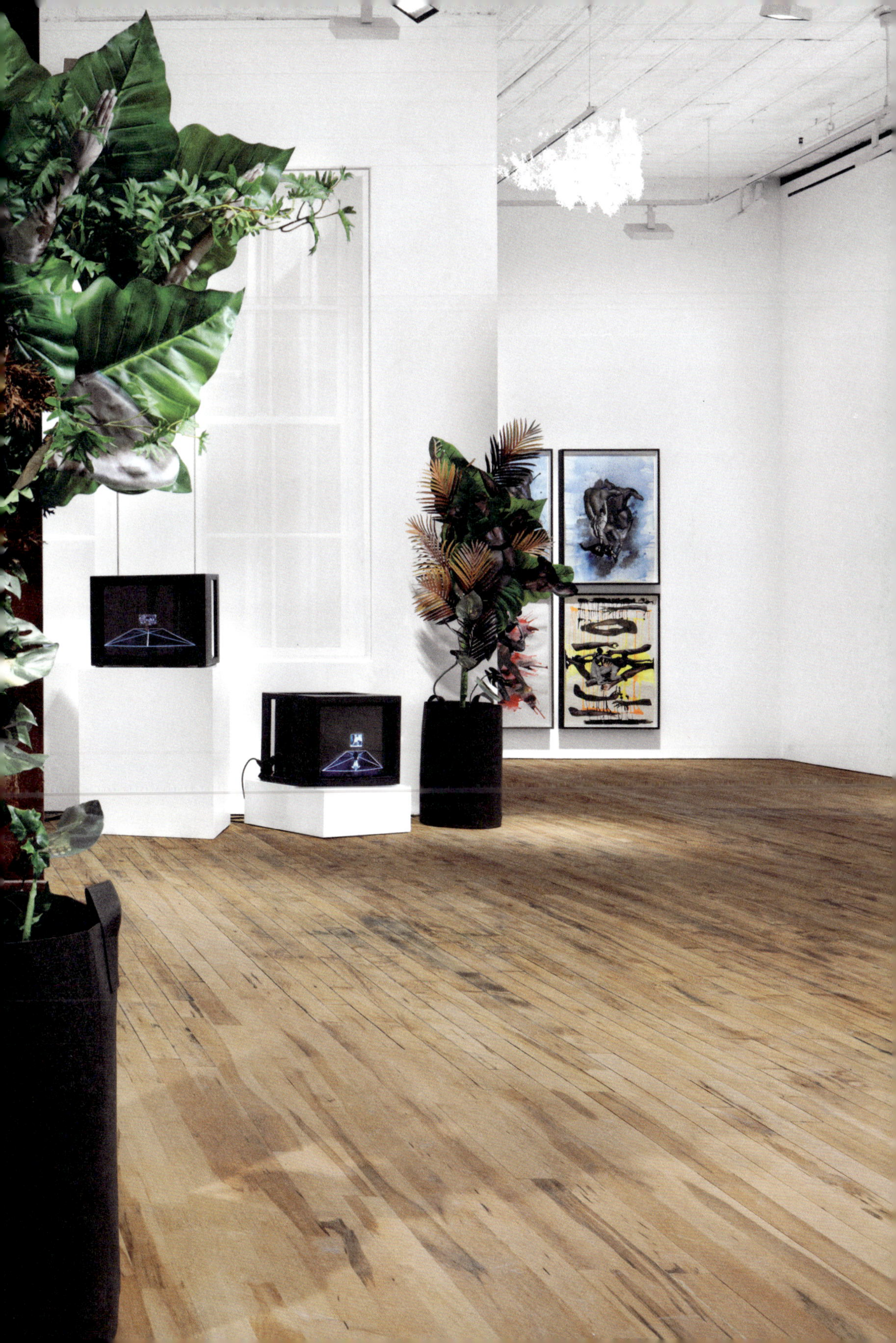

Genes, not Genius: Another aspect of the colonial educational and cultural patterns which needs investigation was expressed not only by hostility to African culture but by paternalism and by praise of negative and static social features. There were many colonialists who wished to preserve in perpetuity everything that was African, if it appeared quaint or intriguing to them, 2021
Collage on artificial plant, fabric grow bag with moss, acrylic paint, and plastic
95 × 48 × 33 inches | 241.3 × 121.9 × 83.8 cm

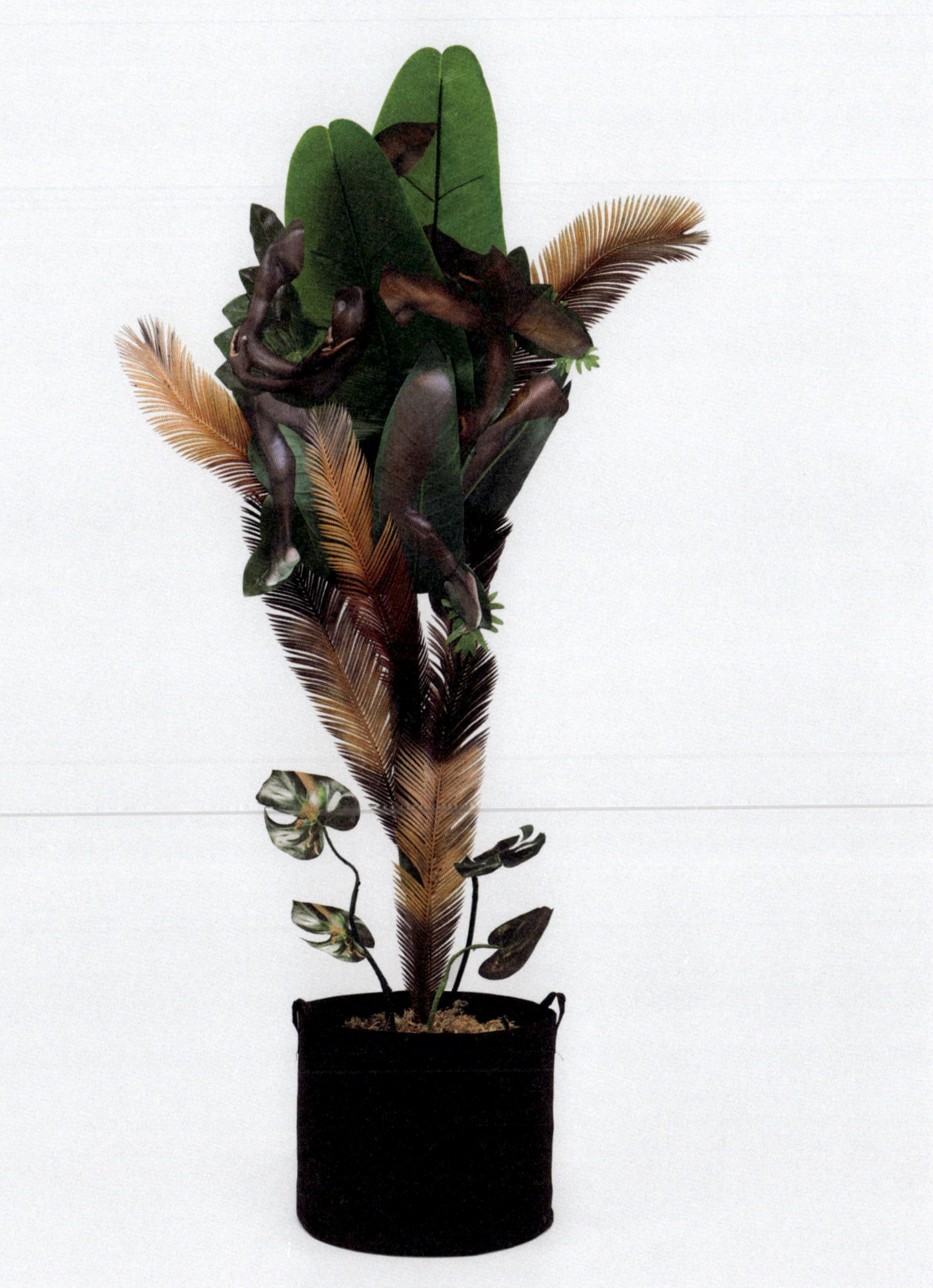

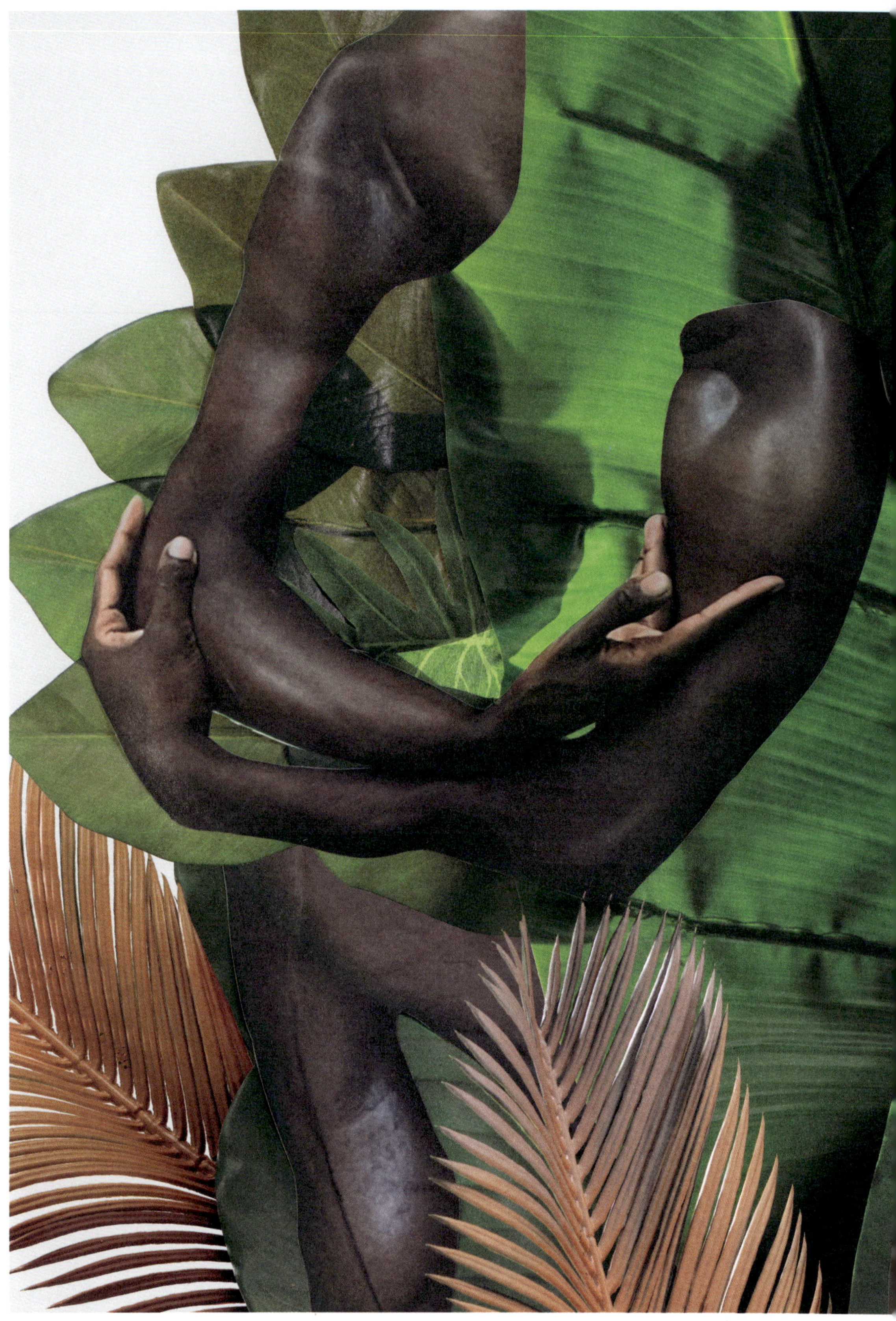

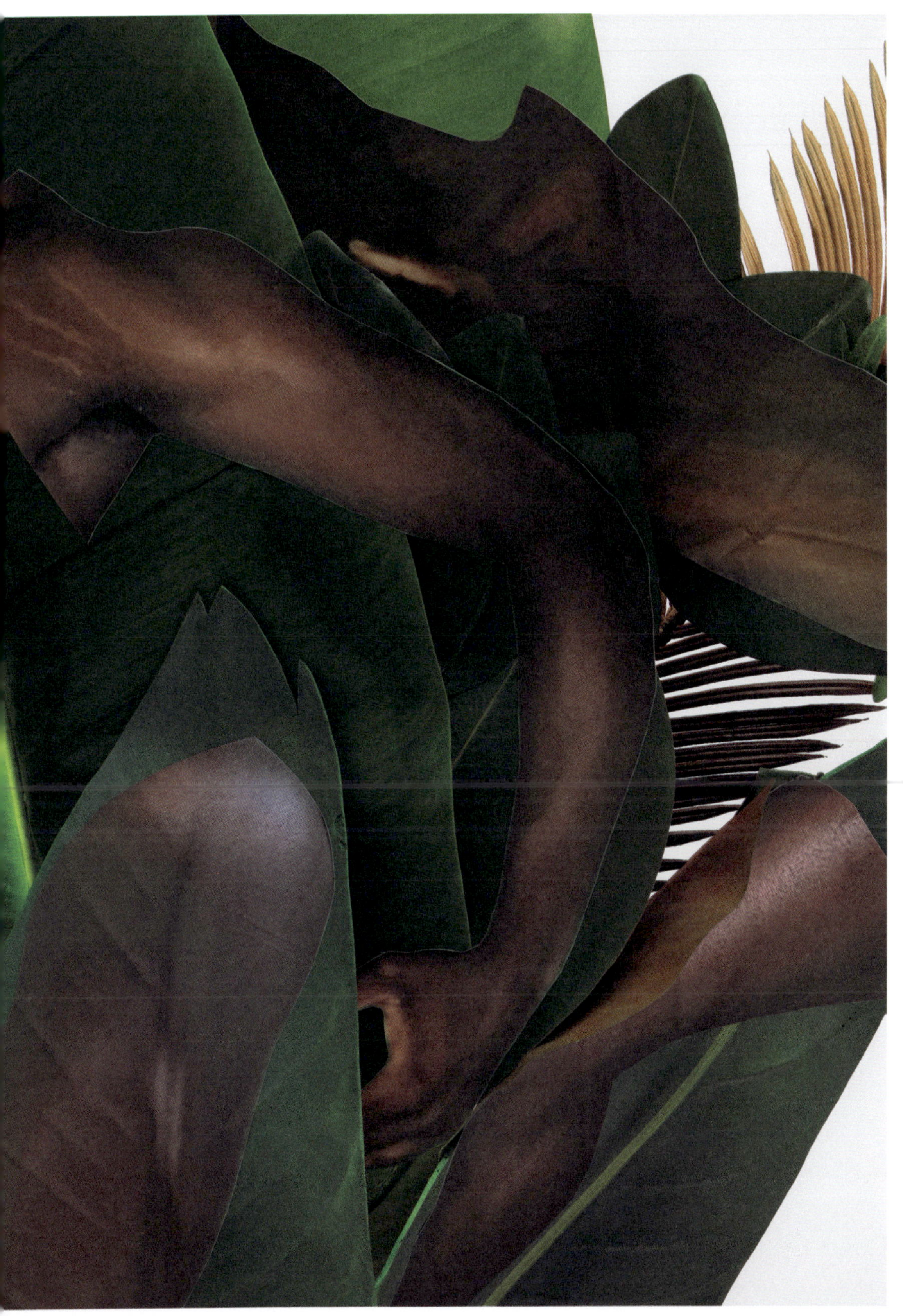

On the contrary, a legend gradually formed, which was neither investigated nor questioned. The legend covered the past with a blanket of oblivion: there had been no modern dance, it seems, under the Nazis, just a bit of ballet at the most. Modern German Dance, the so-called Ausdruckstanz, Expressive Dance, it was claimed, belonged to the great tradition of the artistic avant-garde in the early 20th century and hence was by definition progressive. Each instance of its performance according to how well it manifests the intention and the detail of the choreography, might then be thought to have a form outside of performance and that form pre-exists any written documents. Writing about and on behalf of black artists, Locke refused the responsibilities and limits of politics in artwork in favor of "expression." He argued that the purpose of black artwork was not to correct white supremacist misrepresentations of black life or history or to "demonstrate" that black people were, in fact, worthy of social and political inclusion. (That he took for granted, just as he should have.) Rather, Locke thought that (black) artwork should be "expressive of" "Negro life," in all its variety and vitality. Expressiveness was for Locke the mark of the most successful modern art, 2021
Collage on artificial plant, fabric grow bag with moss, acrylic paint, and plastic
98 × 42 × 36 inches | 248.9 × 106.7 × 91.4 cm

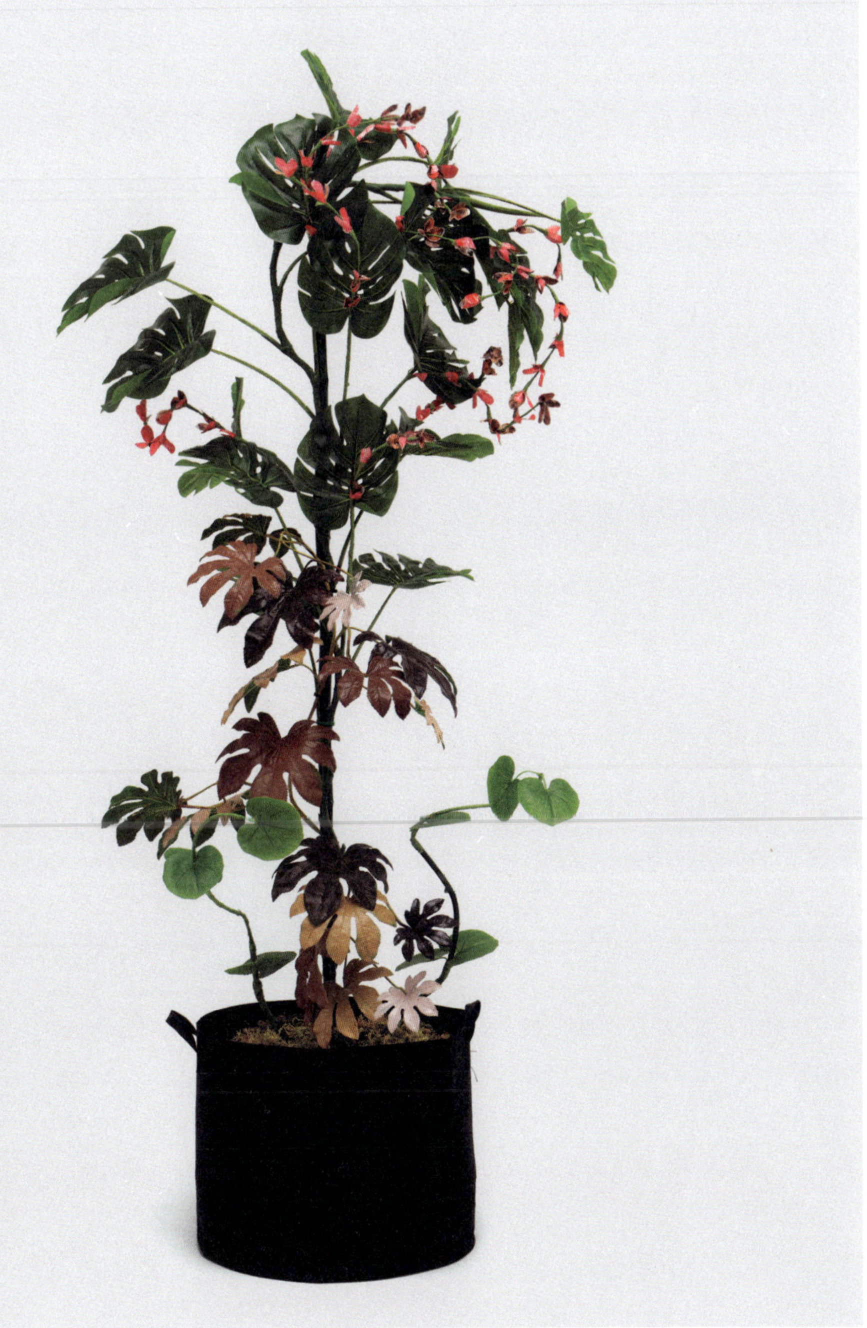

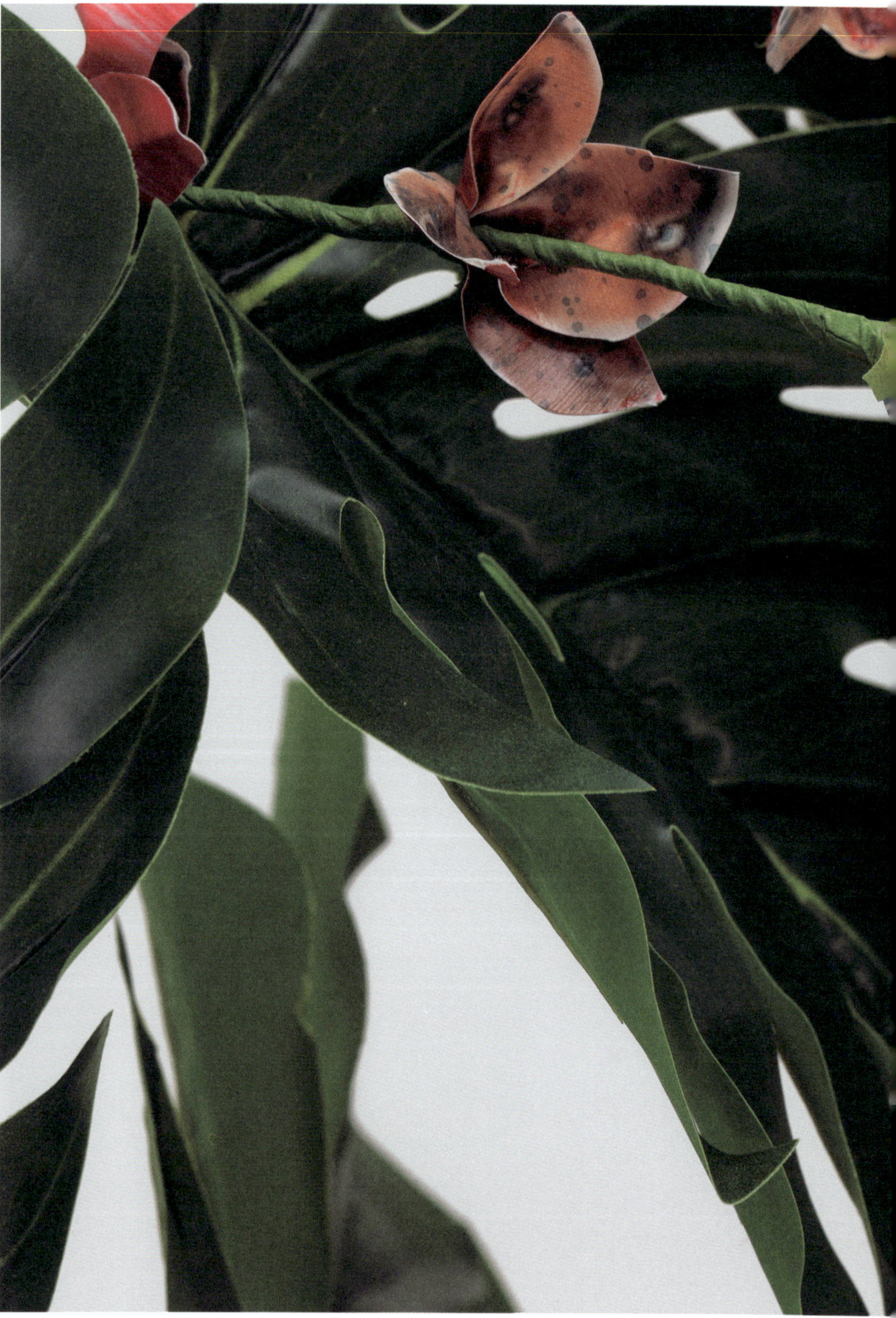

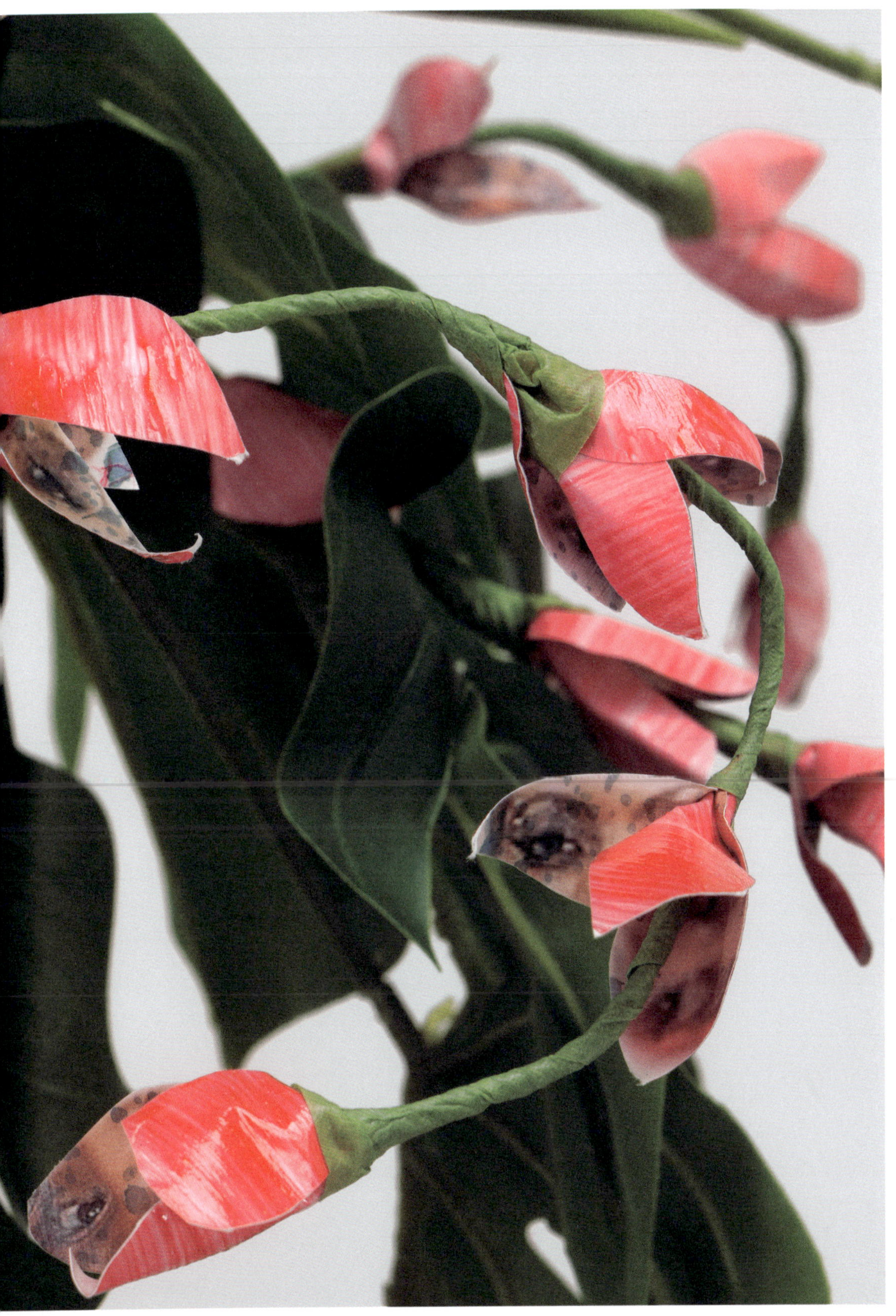

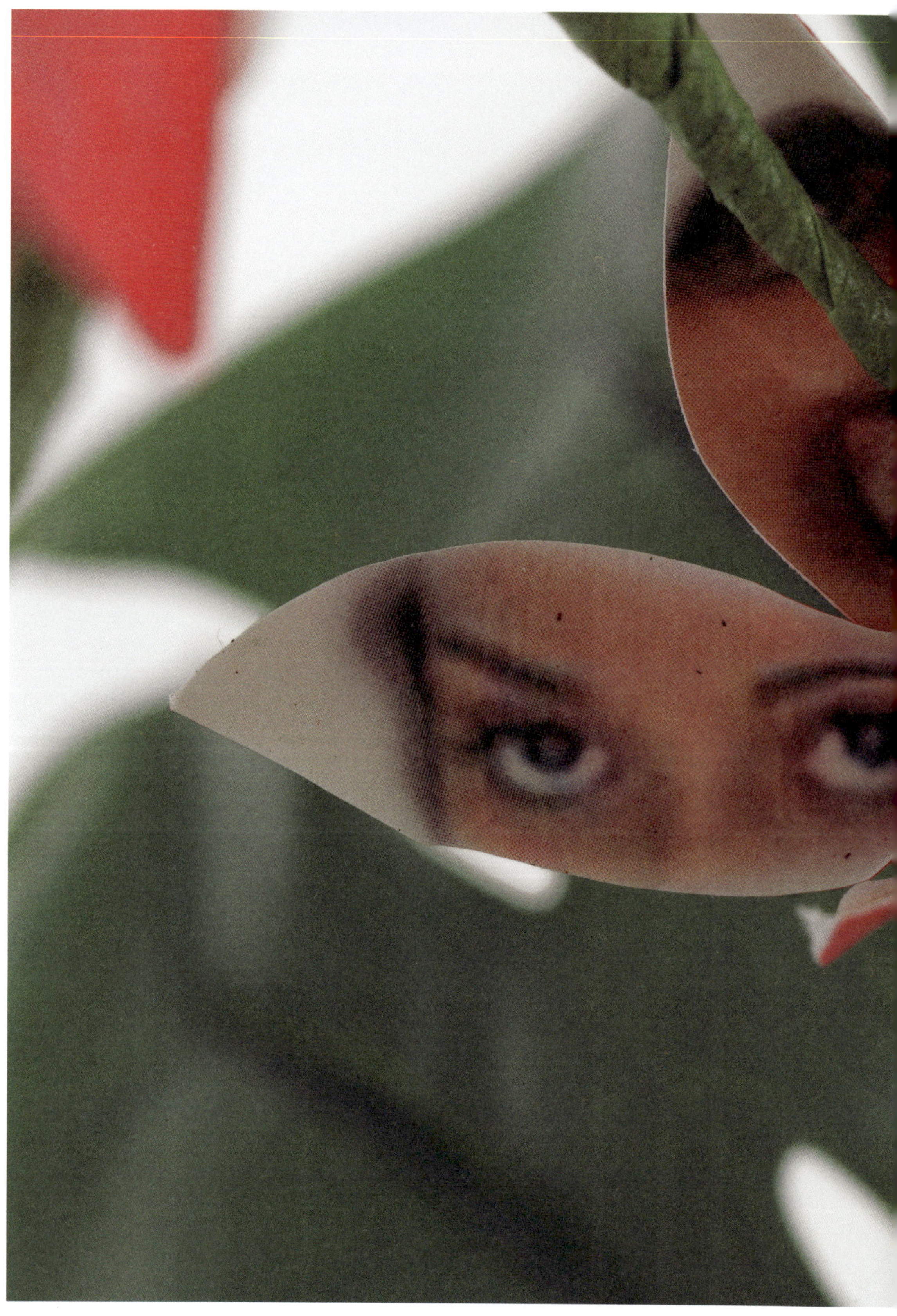

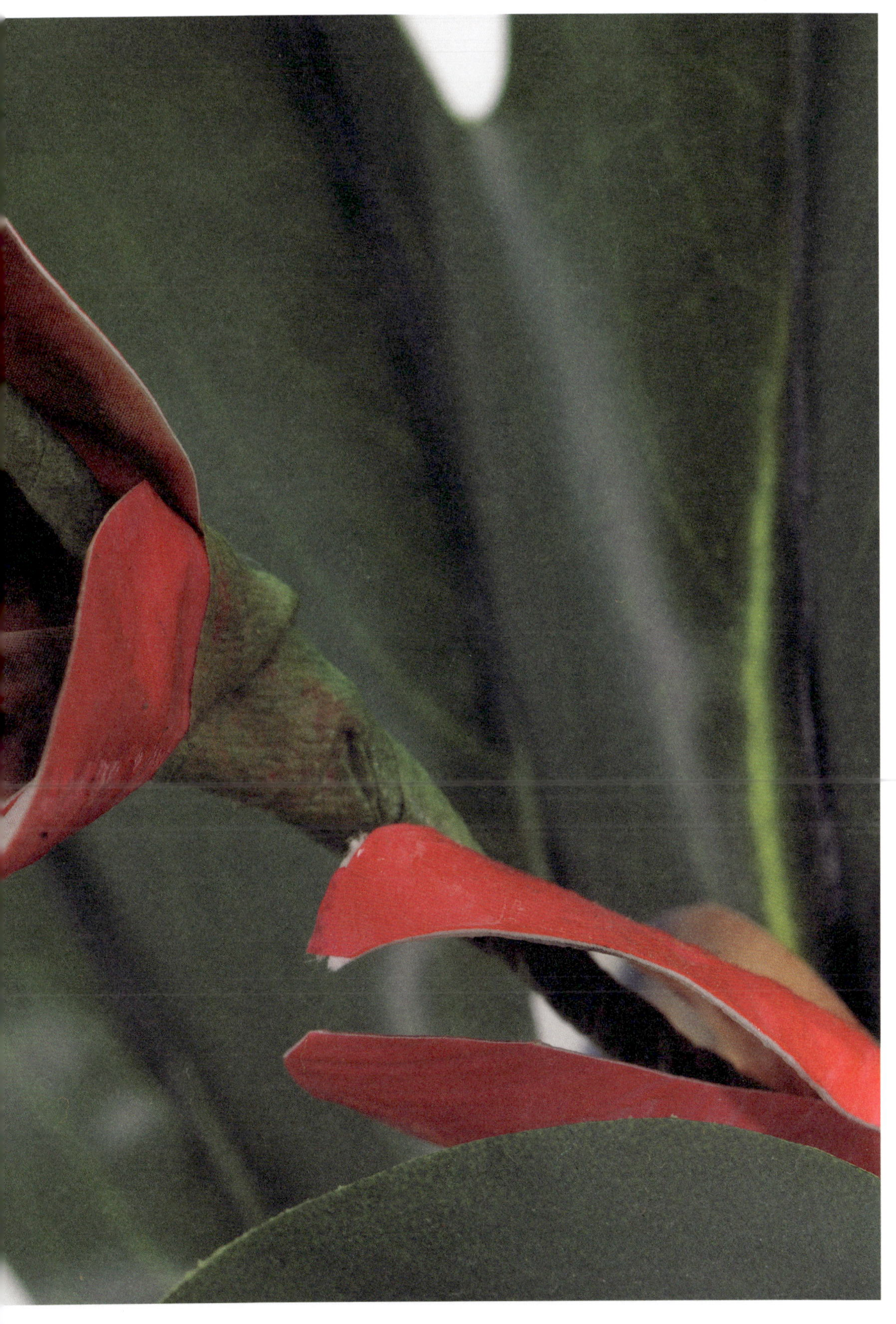

"Britannica" now: choreography, the art of creating and arranging dances. The word derives from the Greek for "dance" and for "write." In the 17th and 18th centuries, it did indeed mean the written record of dances. In the 19th and 20th centuries, however, the meaning shifted, inaccurately but universally, while the written record came to be known as dance notation. In biological taxonomy, race is an informal rank in the taxonomic hierarchy for which various definitions exist. Sometimes it is used to denote a level below that of subspecies, while at other times it is used as a synonym for subspecies. A race is a grouping of humans based on shared physical or social qualities into categories generally viewed as distinct by society.[1] The term was first used to refer to speakers of a common language and then to denote national affiliations. By the 17th century the term began to refer to physical (phenotypical) traits. Modern science regards race as a social construct, an identity which is assigned based on rules made by society.[2] While partially based on physical similarities within groups, race does not have an inherent physical or biological meaning.[1][3][4] Dance notation, the recording of dance movement through the use of written symbols. Dance notation is to dance what musical notation is to music and what the written word is to drama. In dance, notation is the translation of four-dimensional movement (time being the fourth dimension) into signs written on two-dimensional paper. A fifth "dimension"—dynamics, or the quality, texture, and phrasing of movement—should also be considered an integral part of notation, although in most systems it is not, 2021

Artificial plant, fabric grow bag with moss, acrylic paint, and plastic

106 × 33 × 25 inches | 269.2 × 83.8 × 63.5 cm

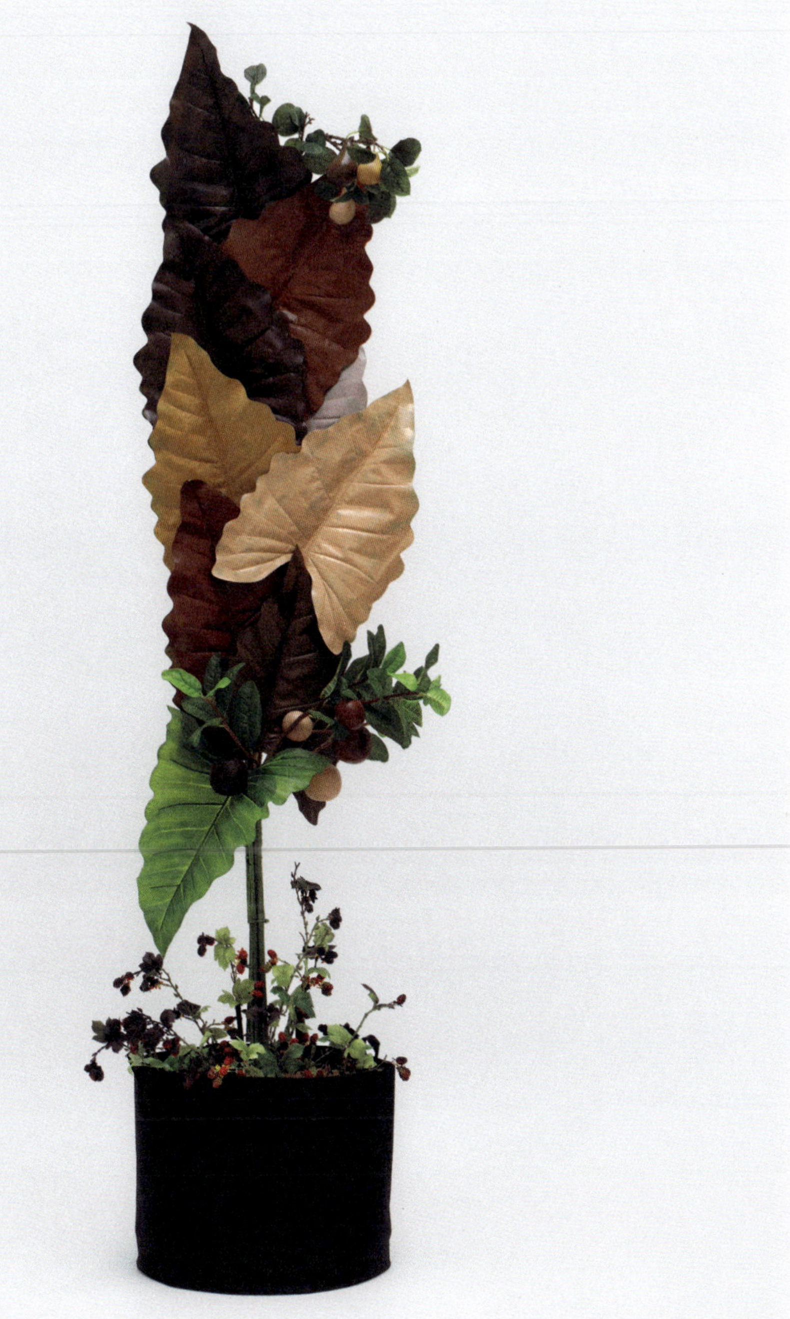

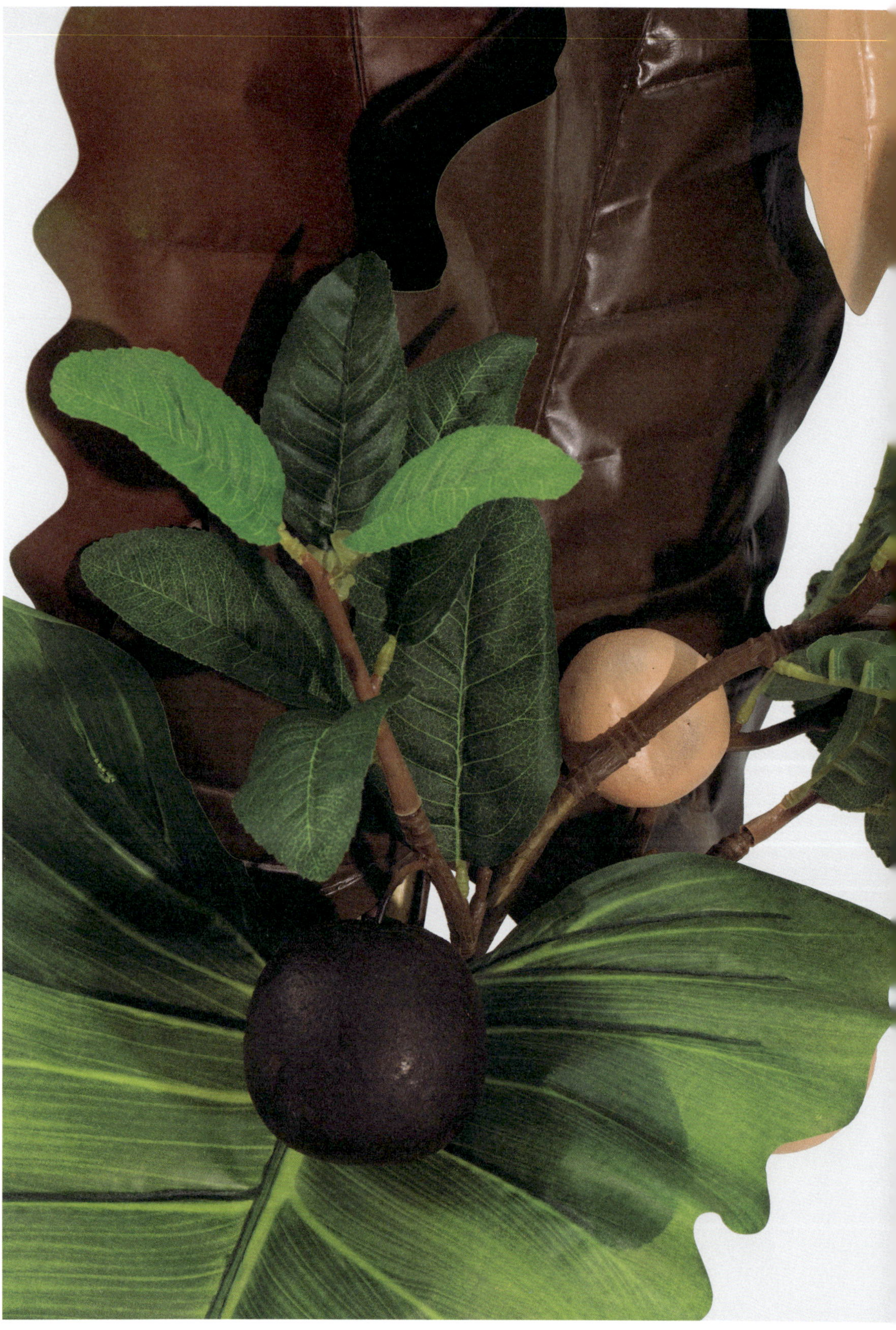

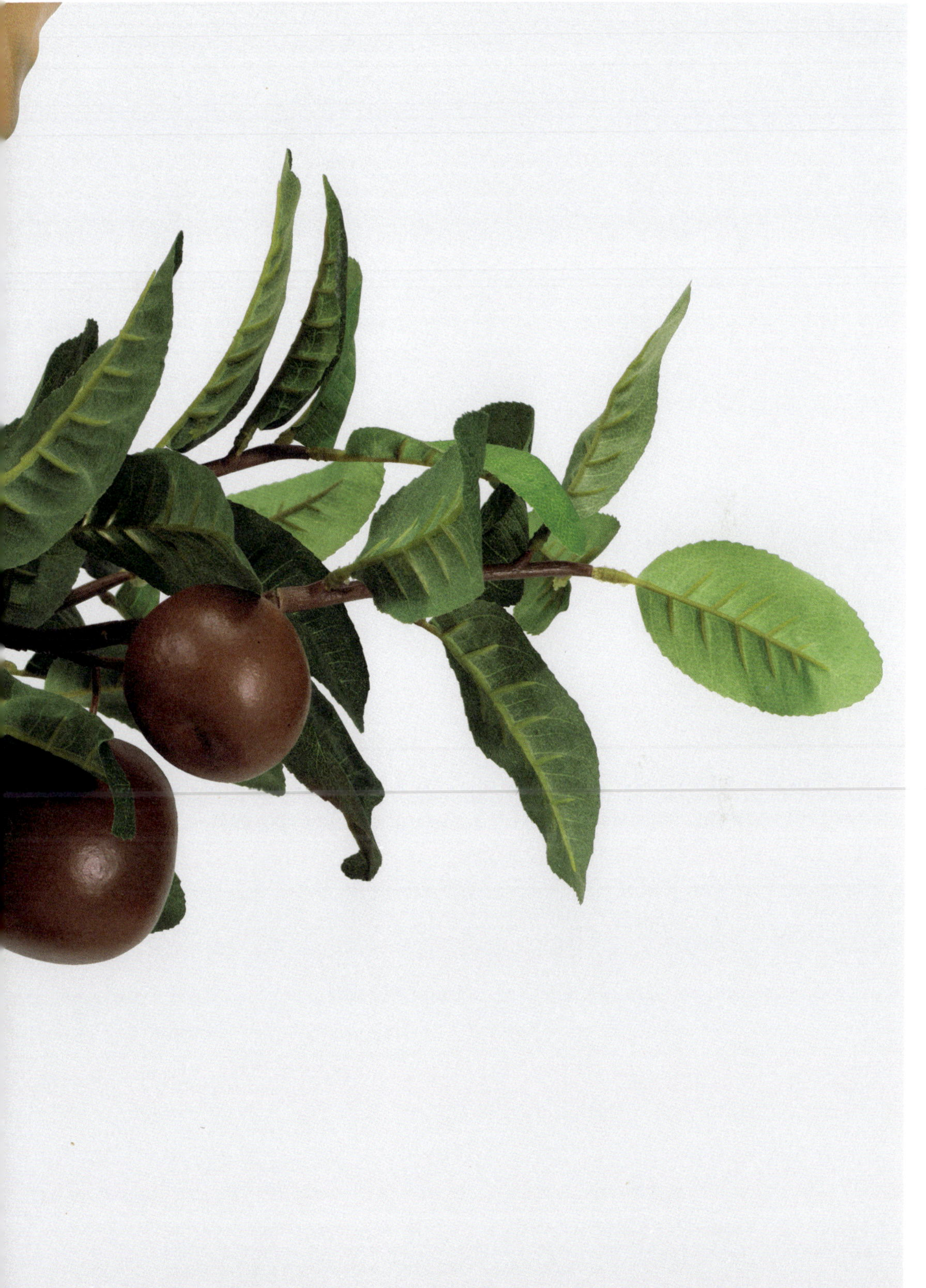

Genes, not Genius: The overlying purpose is to address how the social production of biologically determinist racial scripts—which extend from a biocentric conception of the human—can be dislodged by bringing studies of blackness in/and science into conversation with autopoiesis, black Atlantic livingness, weights and measures, and poetry. A biocentric conception of the human, it should be noted up front, refers to the law-like order of knowledge that posits a Darwinian narrative of the human—that we are purely biological and bioevolutionary beings—as universal; elegance is elimination, 2021

Collage on artificial plant, fabric grow bag with moss, and plastic

92 × 41 × 18 inches | 233.7 × 104.1 × 45.7 cm

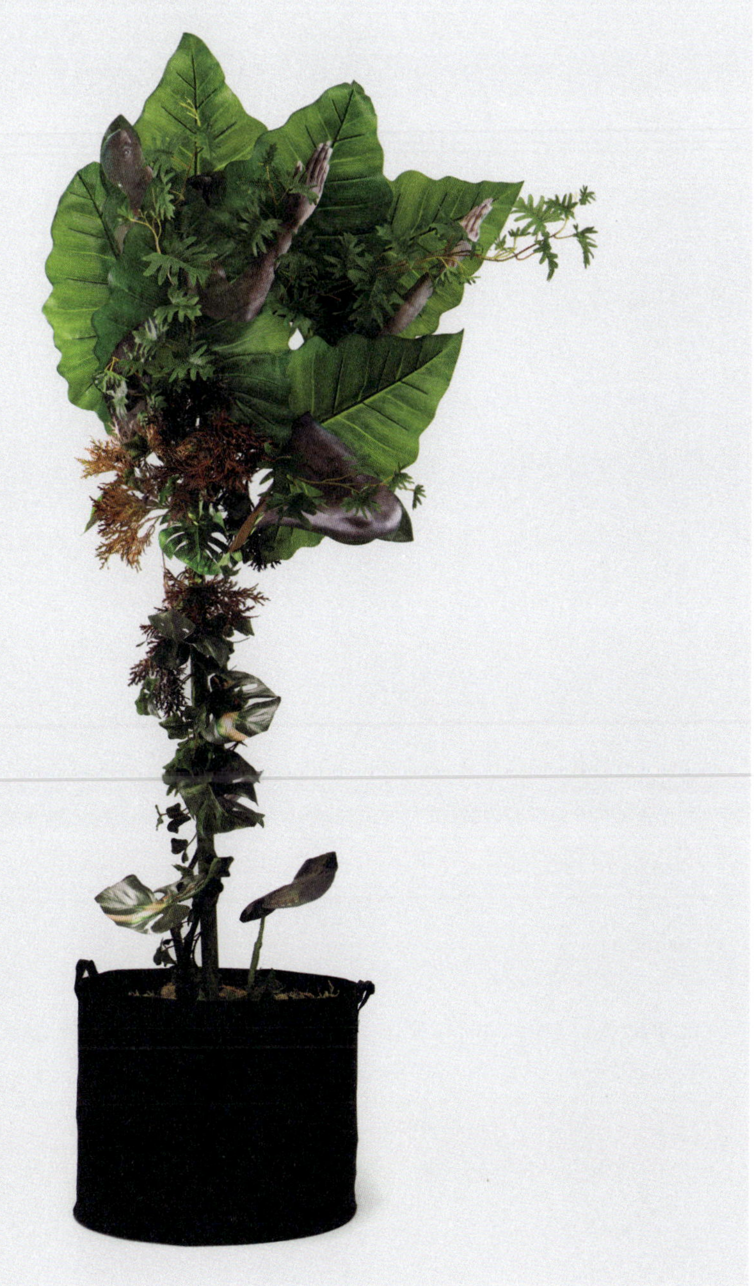

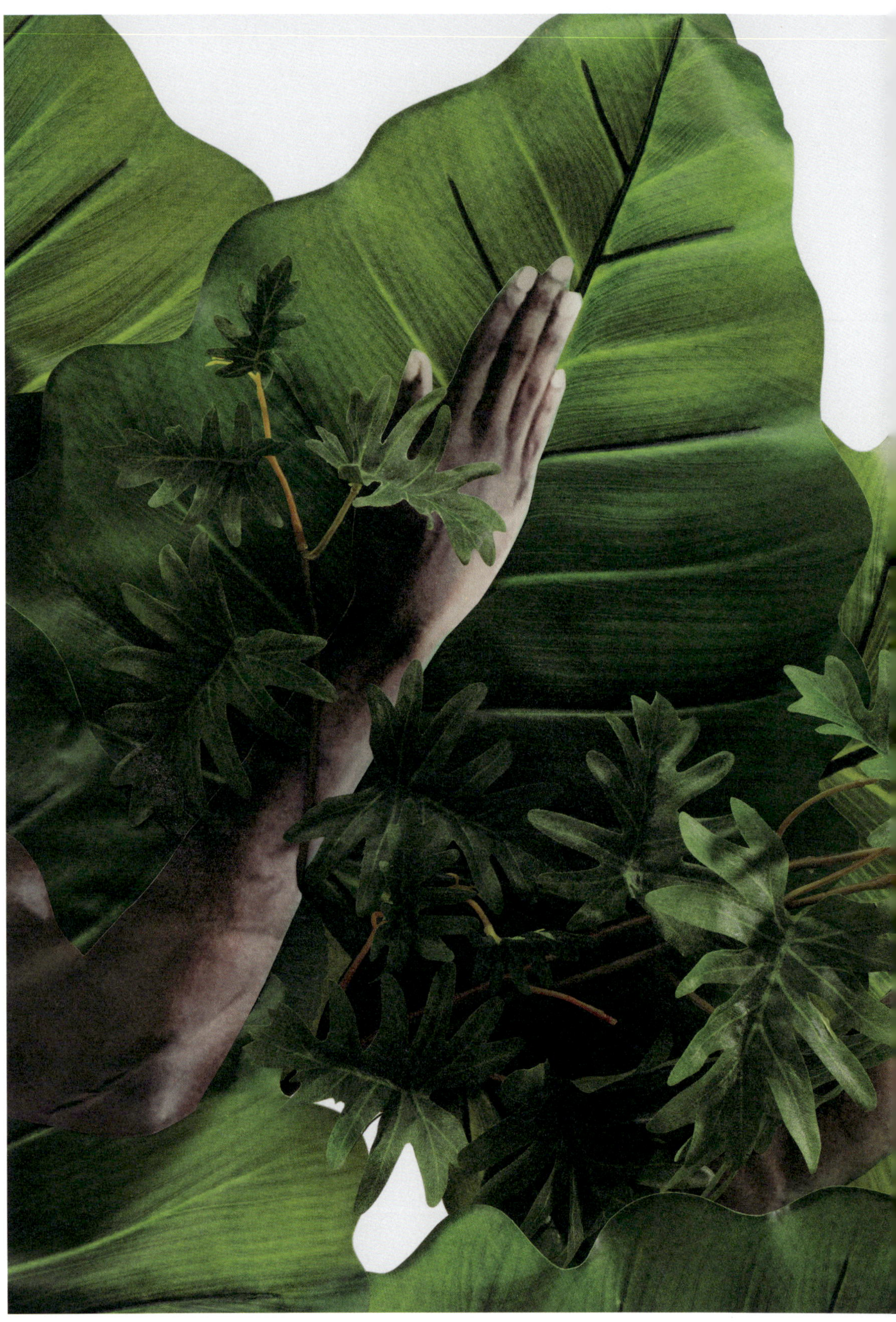

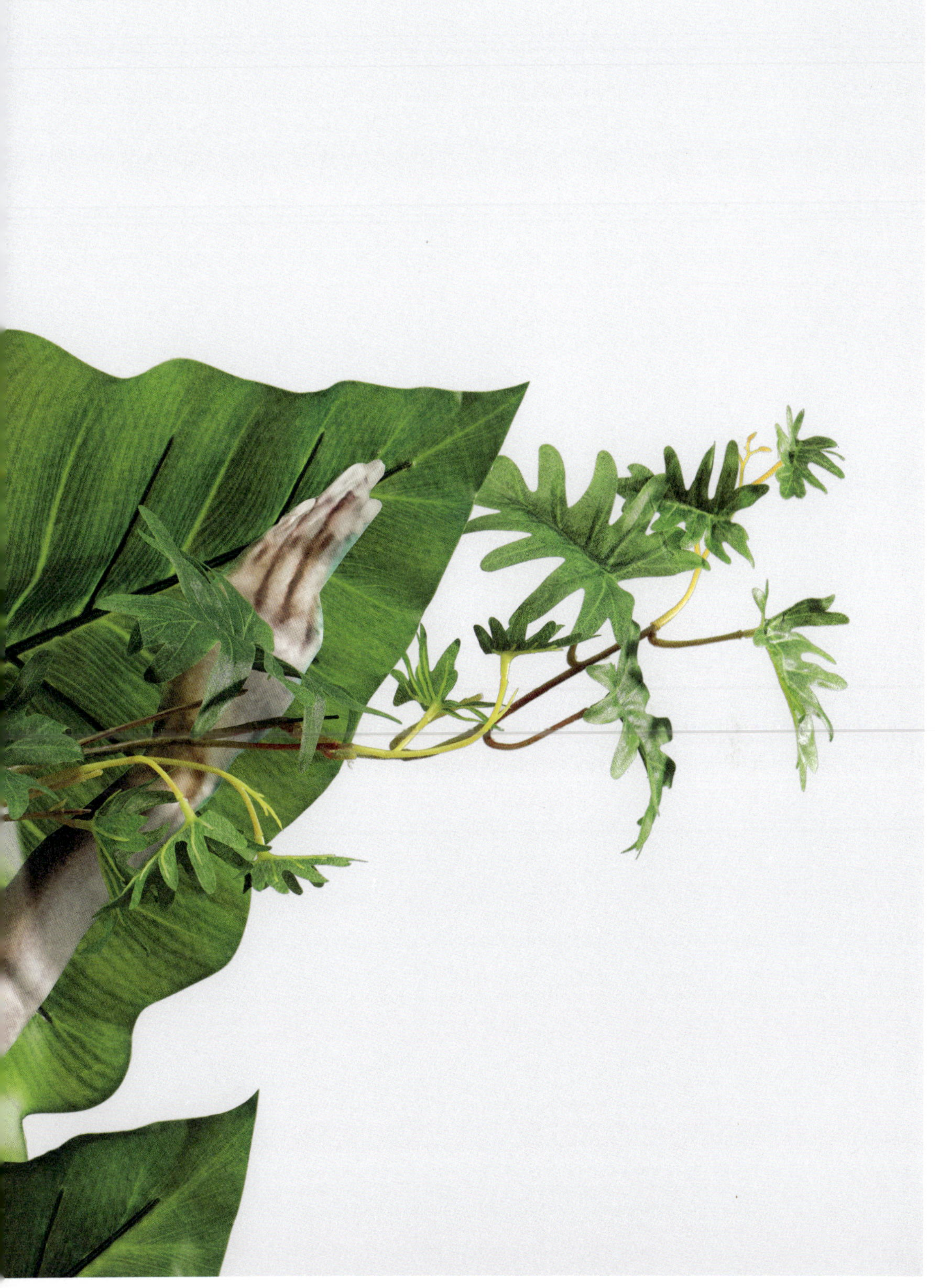

Genes, not Genius: For jazz is orgasm, it is the music of orgasm, good orgasm and bad, and so it spoke across a nation, it had the communication of art even where it was watered, perverted, corrupted, and almost killed, it spoke in no matter what laundered popular way of instantaneous existential states to which some whites could respond, it was indeed a communication by art because it said, "I feel this, and now you do too." Virtuosity is bound to colorism, tokenism, trophyism, and the ruptures of interraciality on legacies of rape and social distortion of dark skin, reverse colorism is not real. The importance of dance in courtship and social gatherings is probably older than its use as recreation and entertainment, 2021
Collage on artificial plant, fabric grow bag with moss, acrylic paint, and plastic
92 × 40 × 20 inches | 233.7 × 101.6 × 50.8 cm

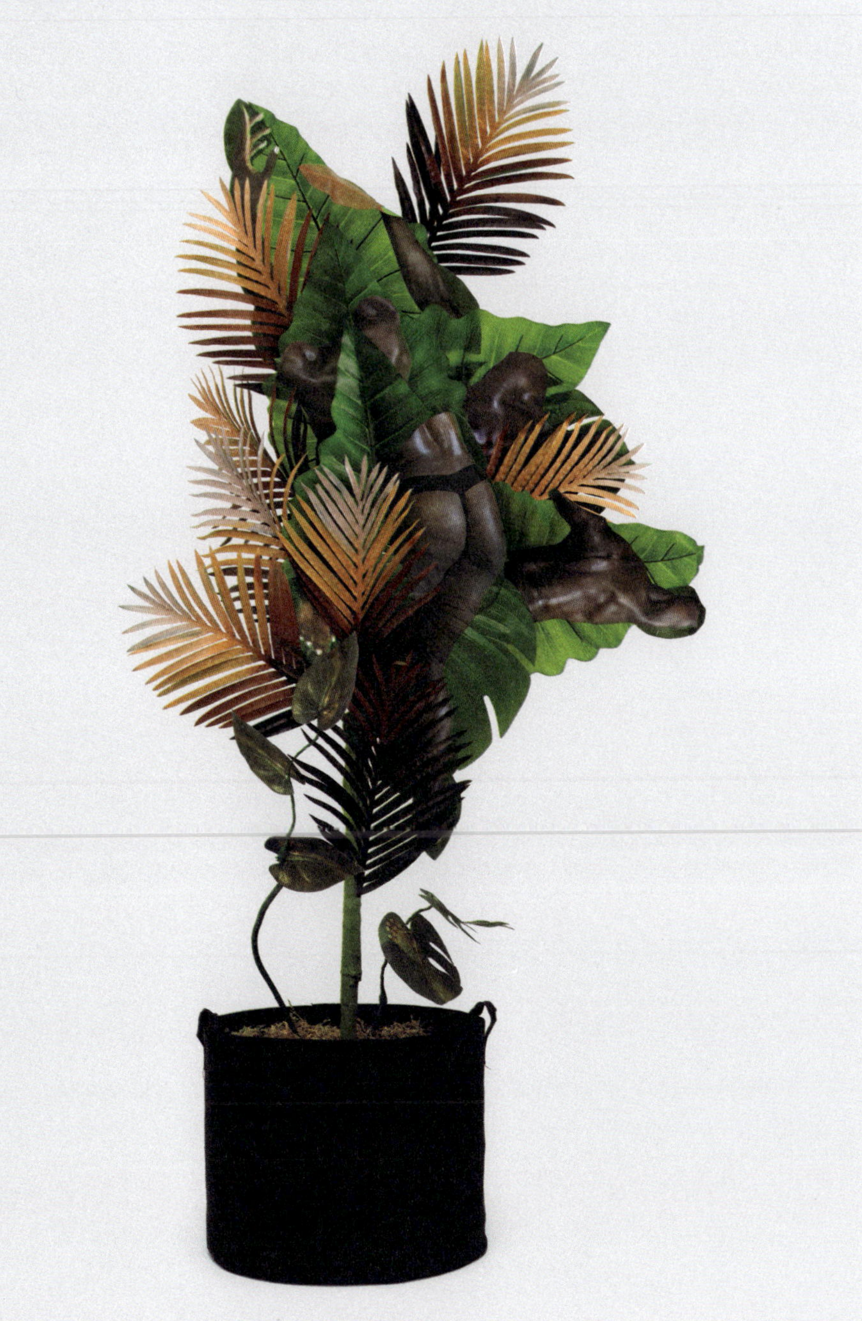

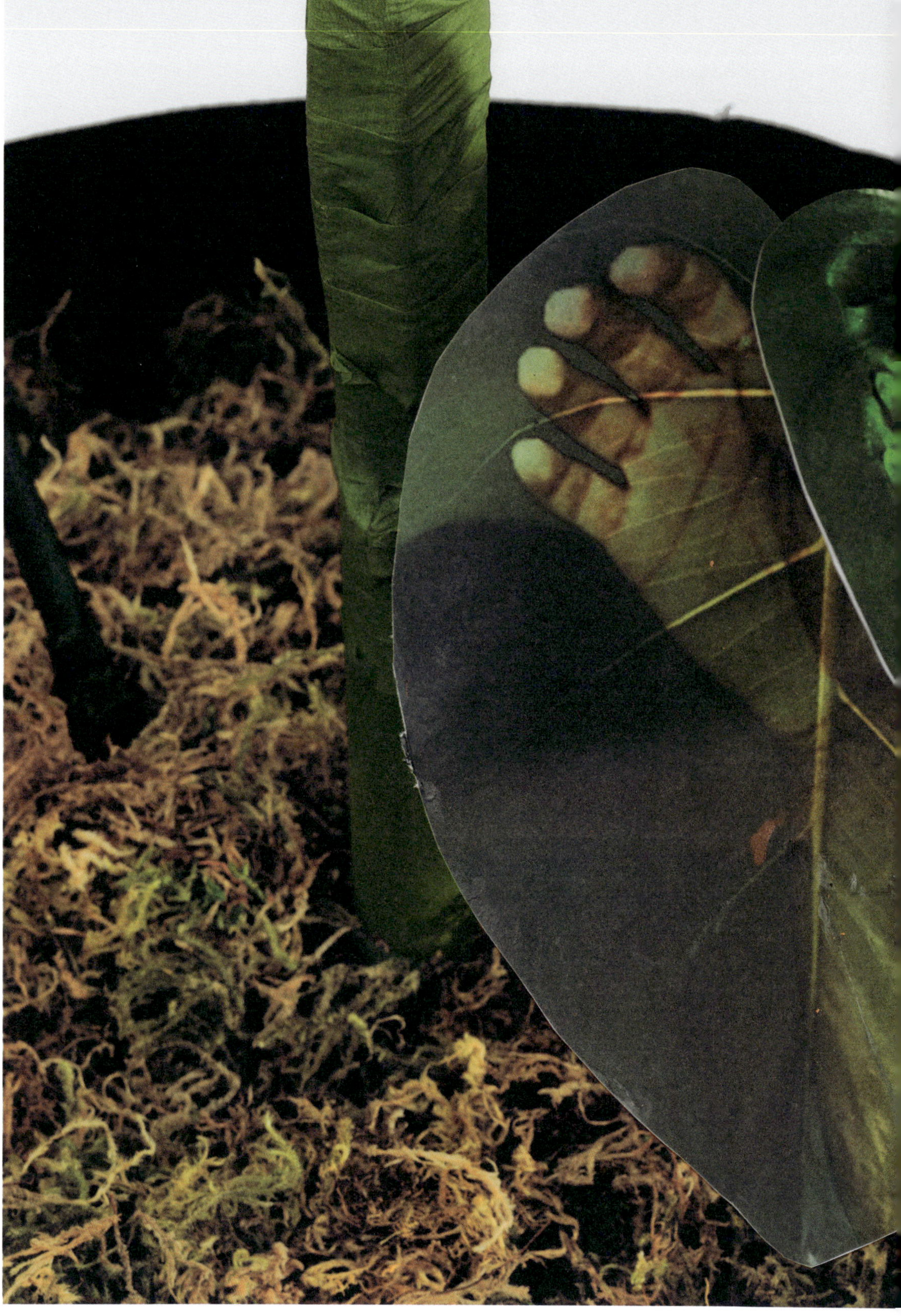

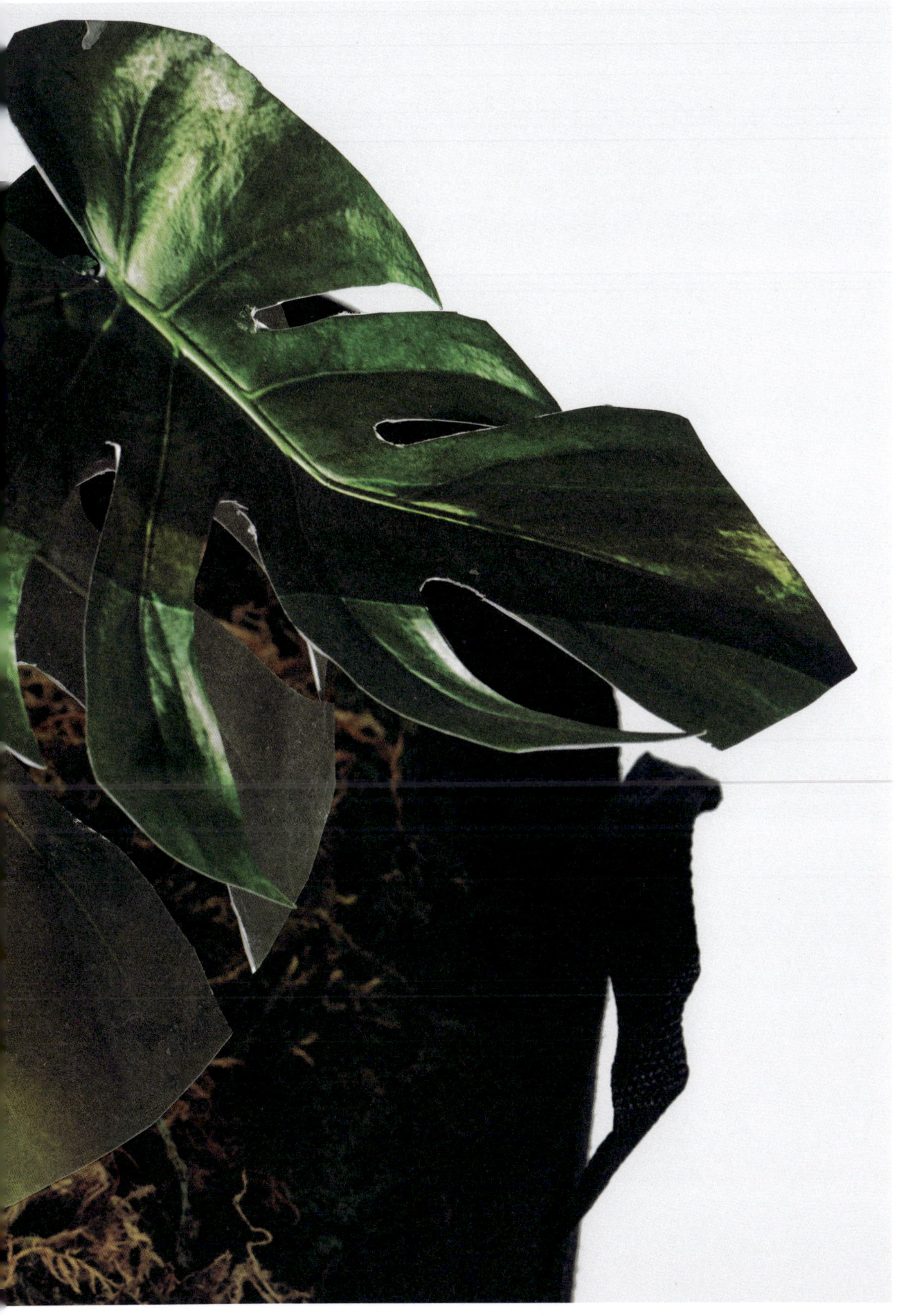

Collage on artificial plant, fabric grow bag with moss, acrylic paint, and plastic
109 × 40 × 18 inches | 276.9 × 101.6 × 45.7 cm

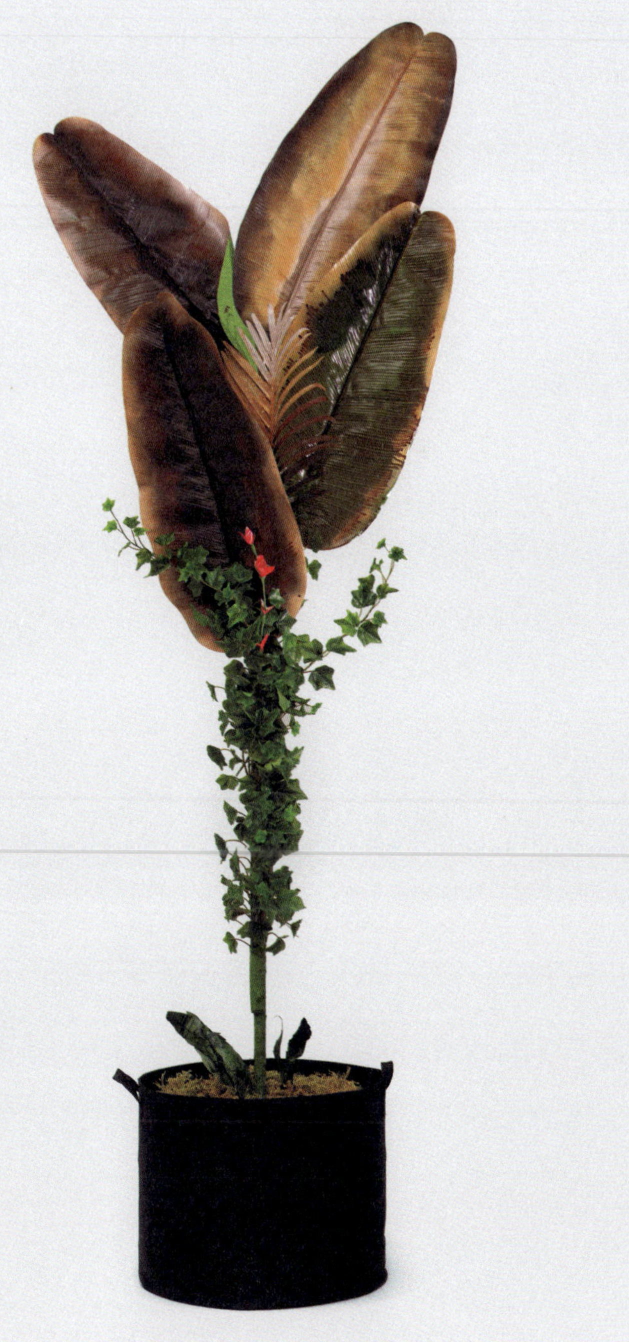

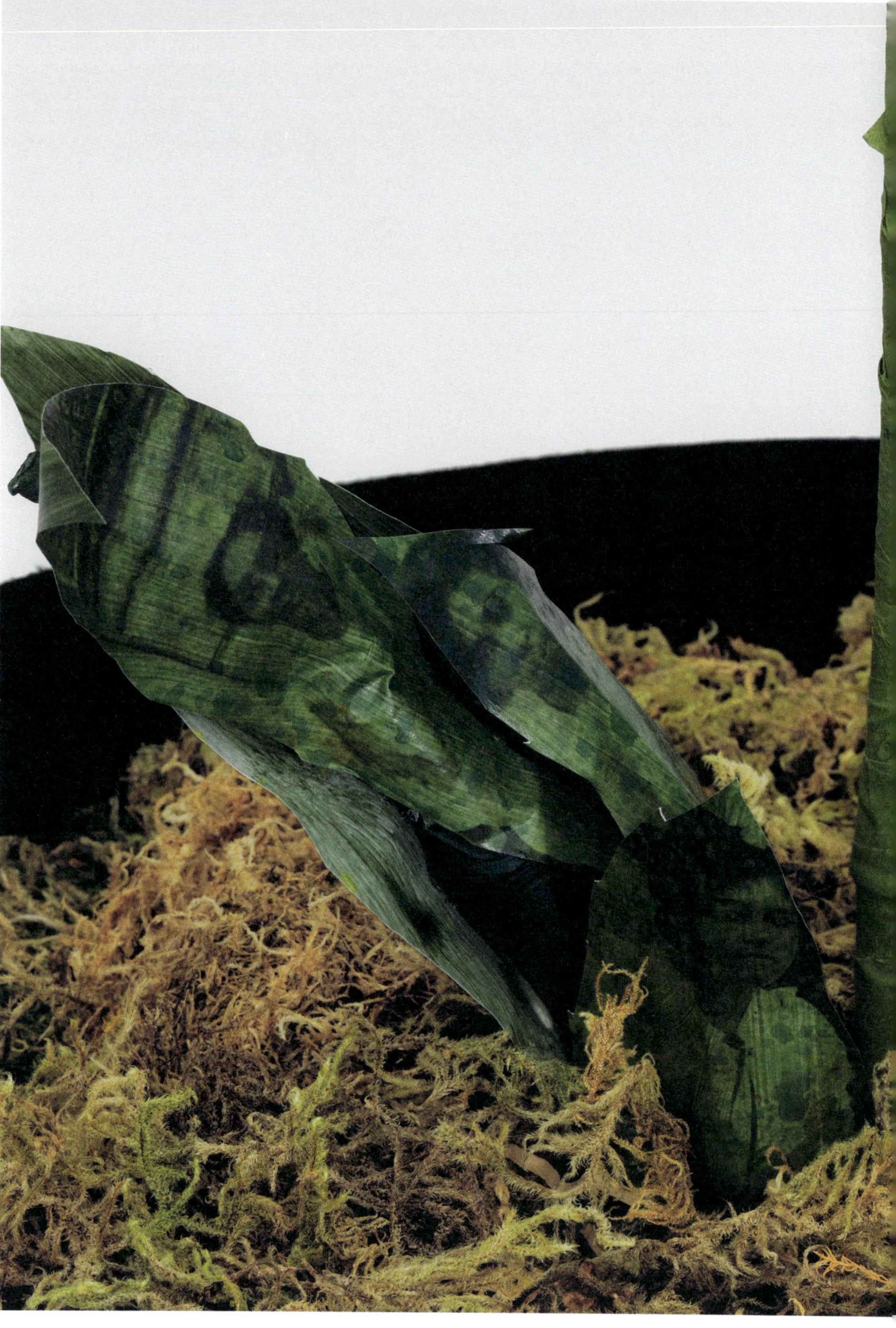

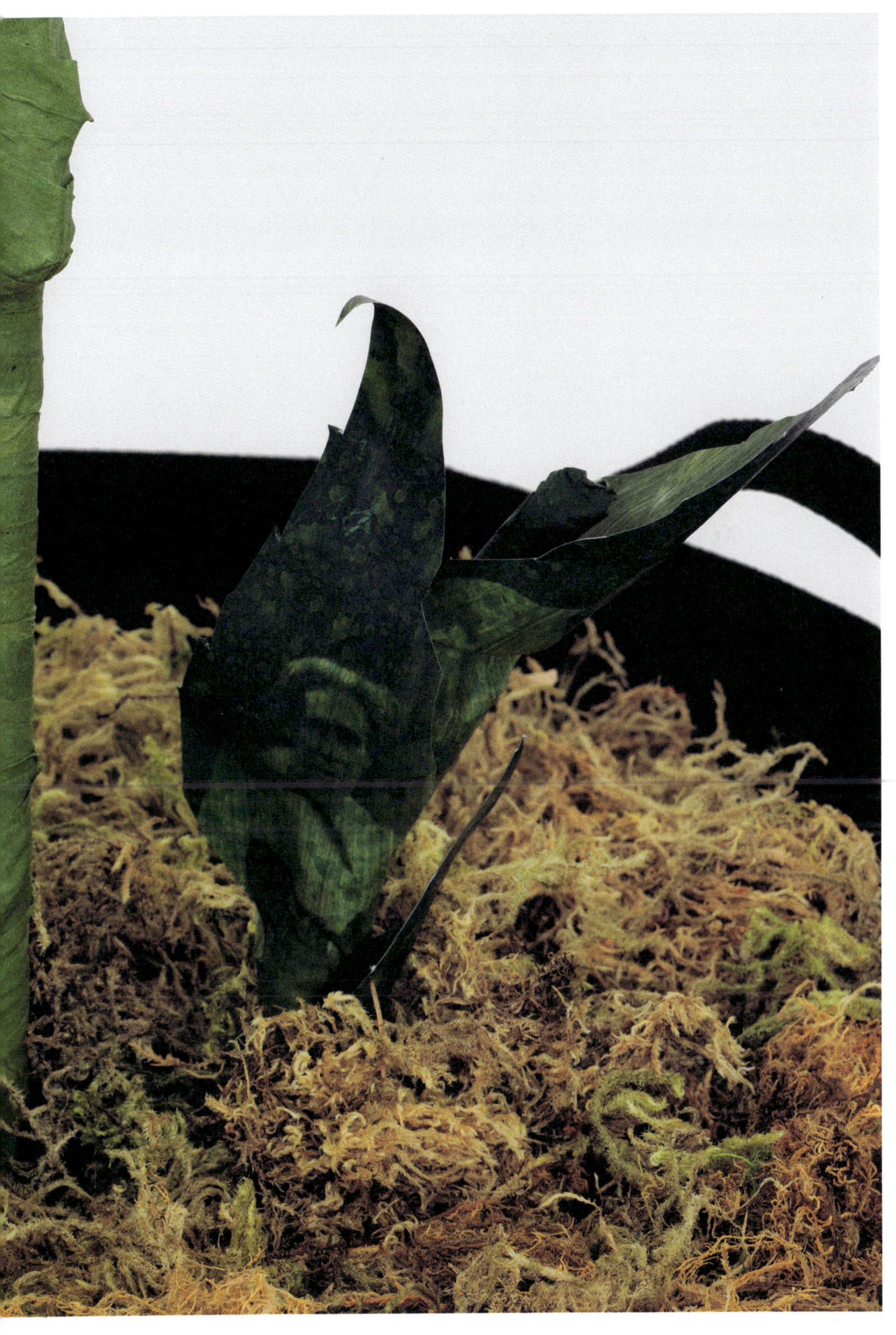

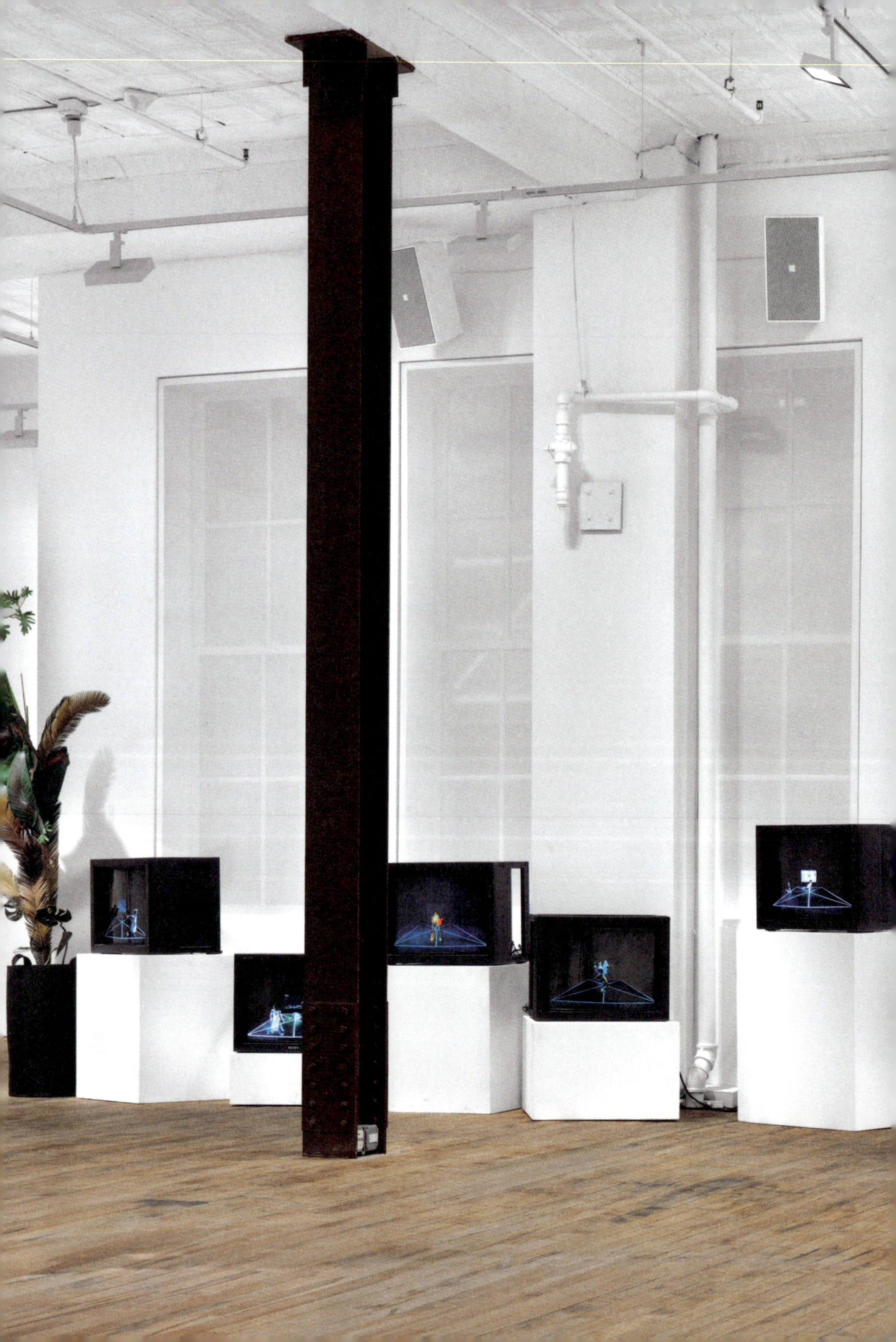

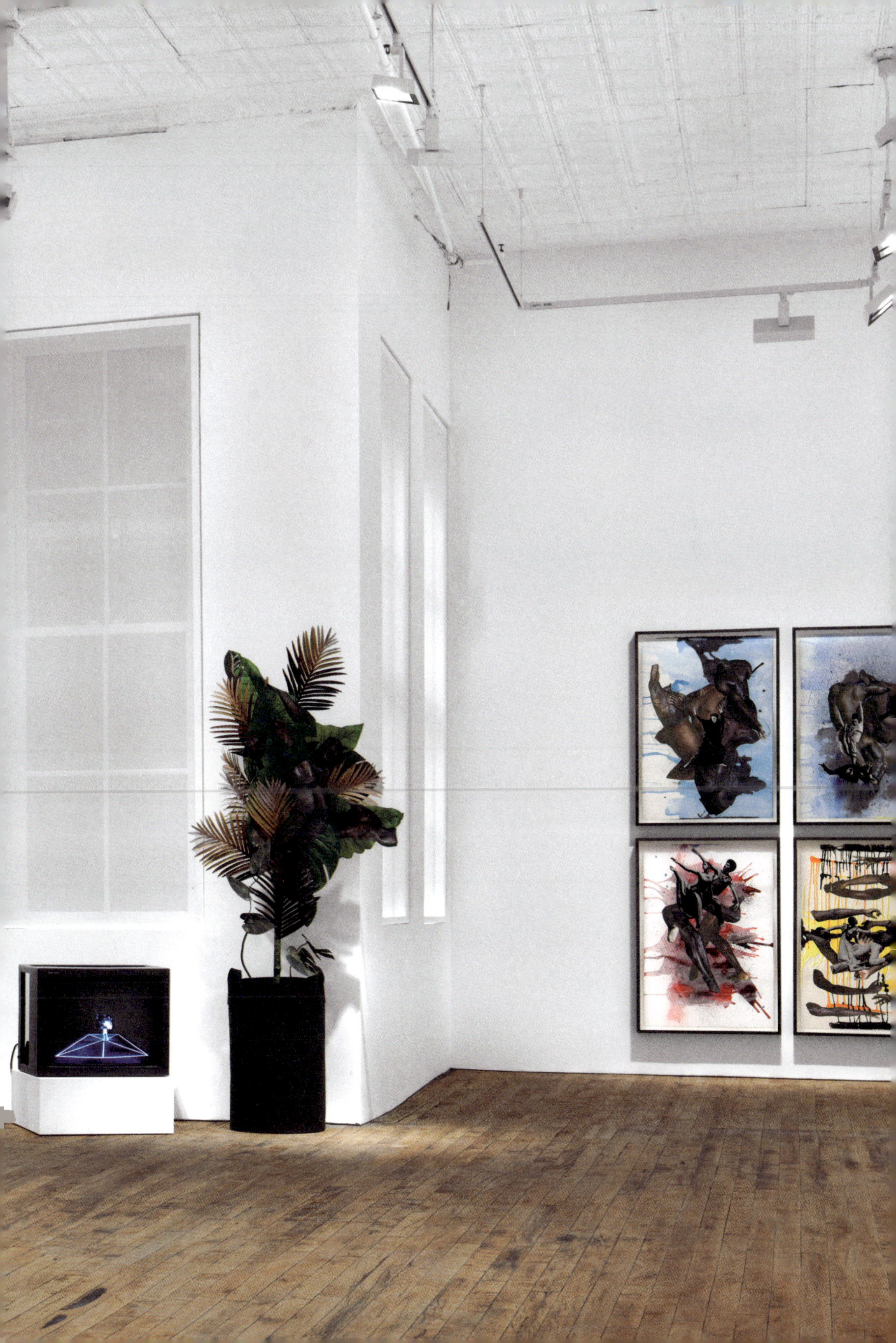

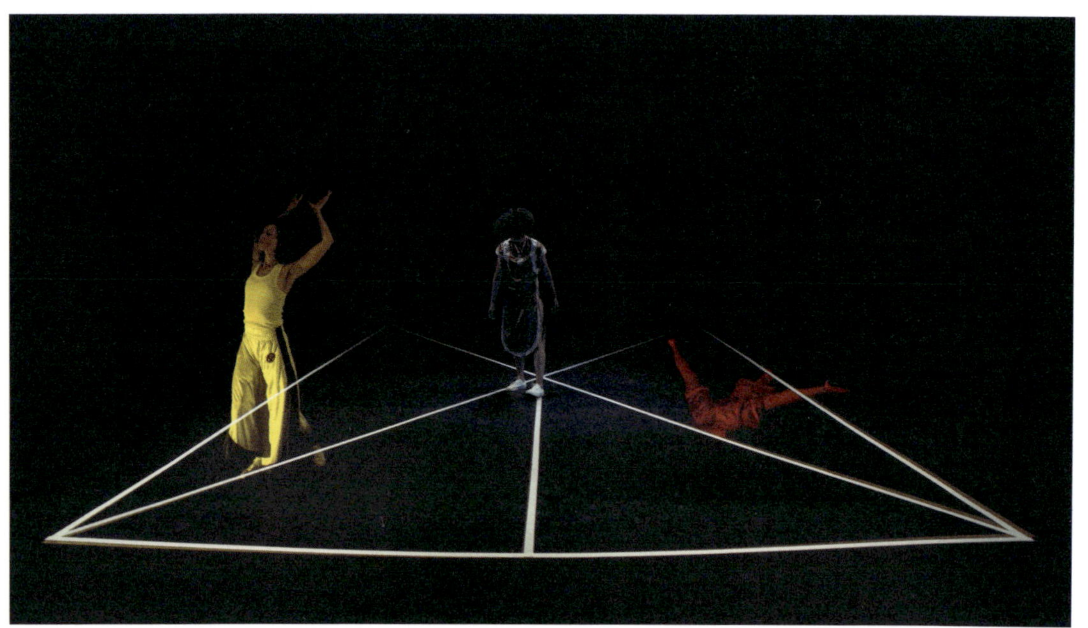

pp. 48–51: Stills from *Triadic Ballet*, 2021
Variable-channel video, variable length, sound
Dimensions variable with installation

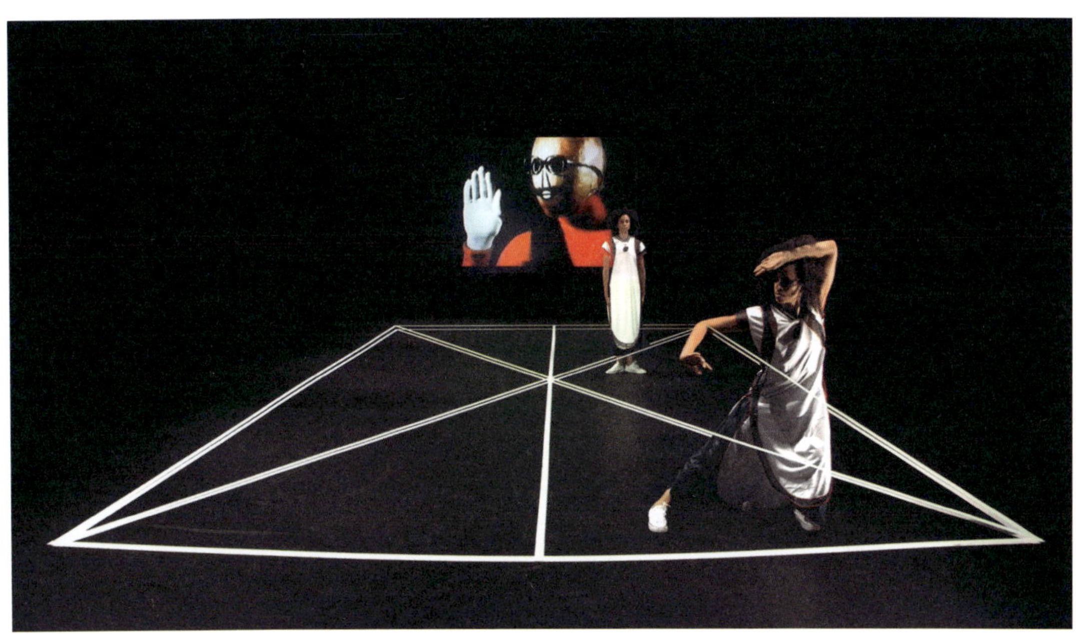

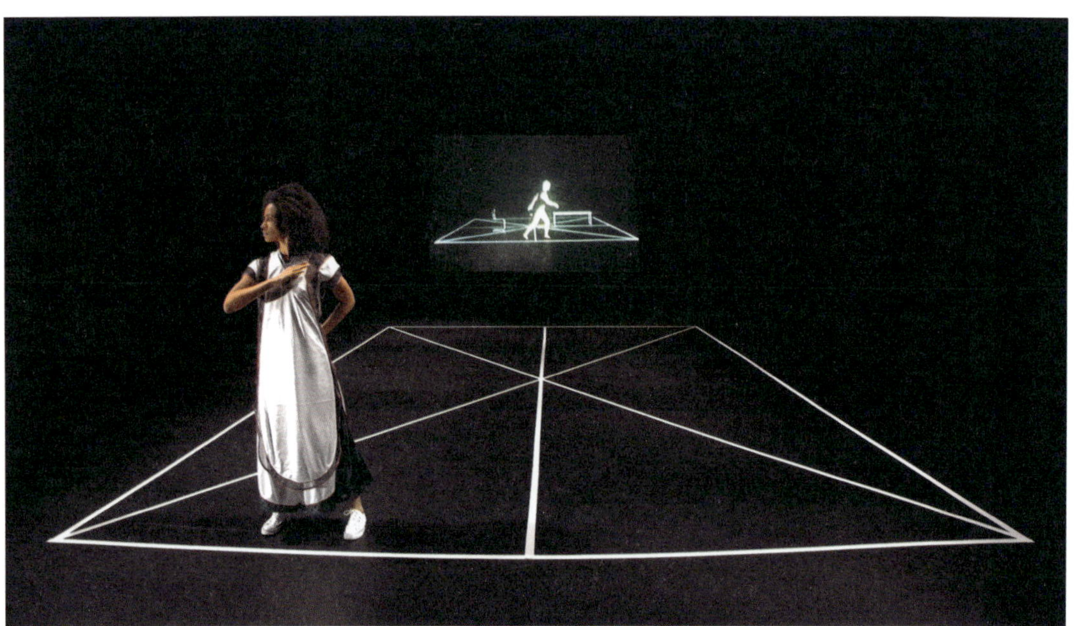

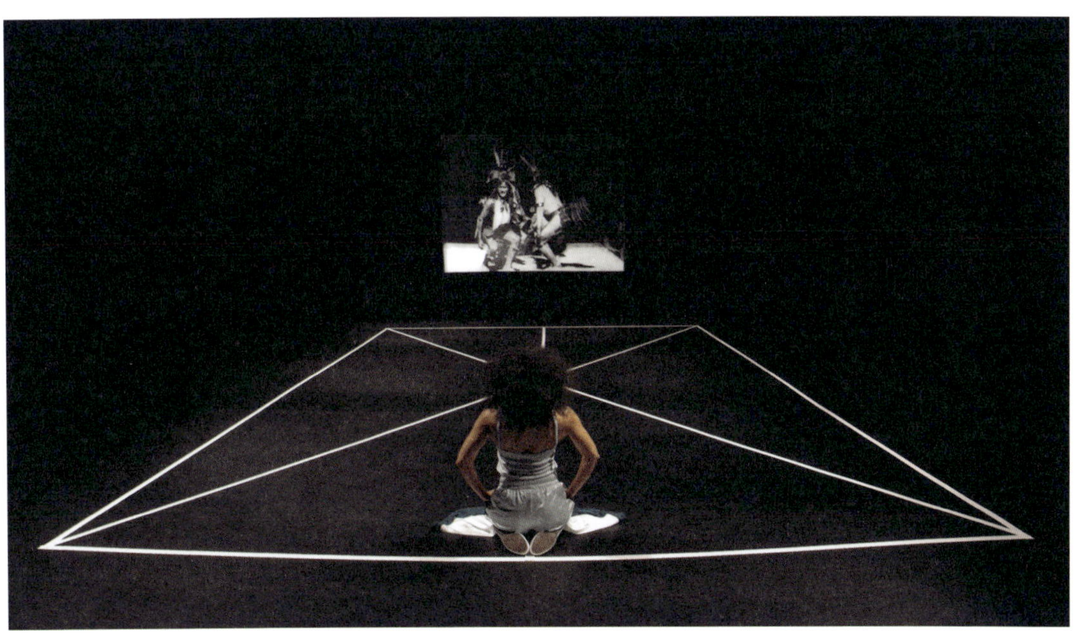

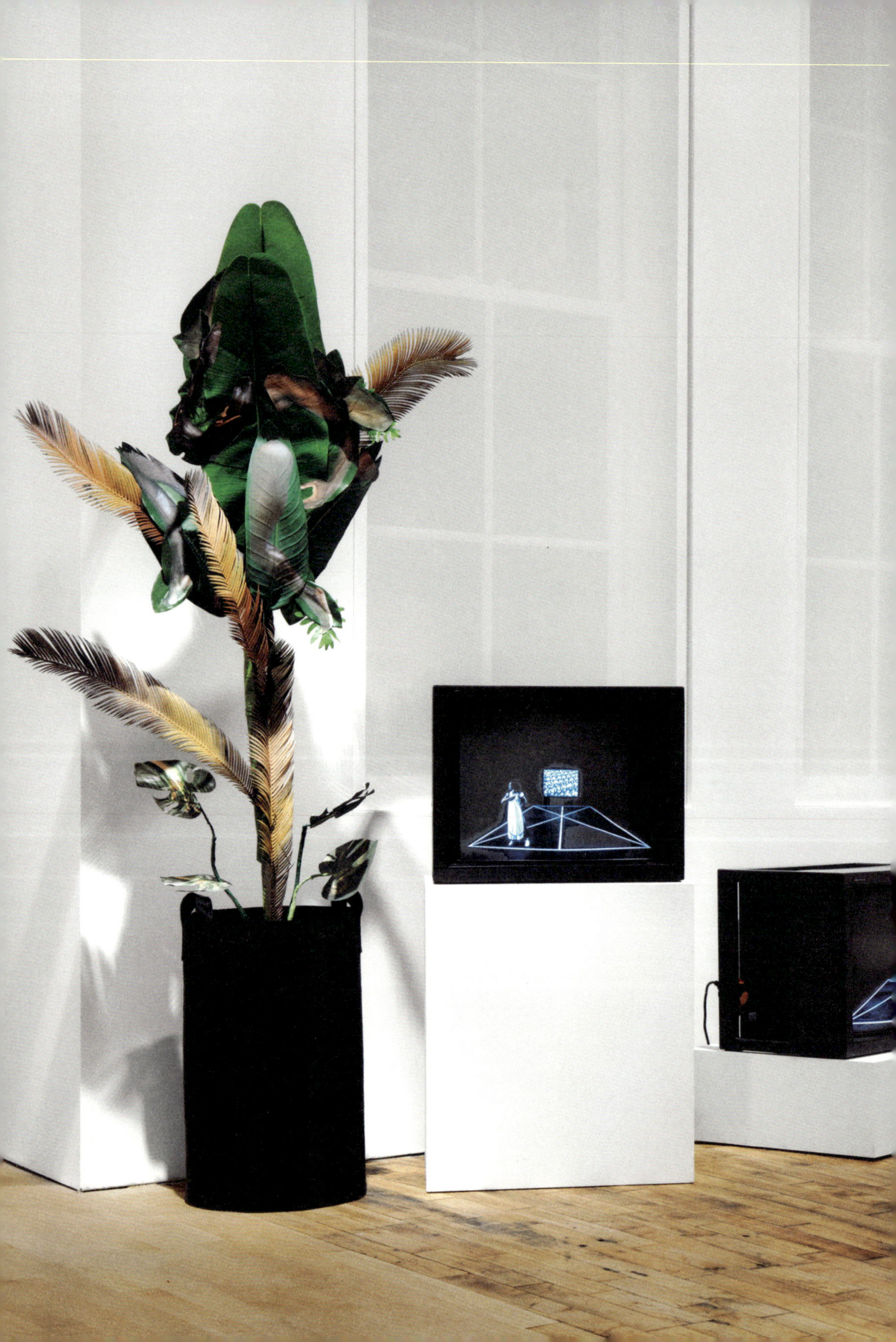

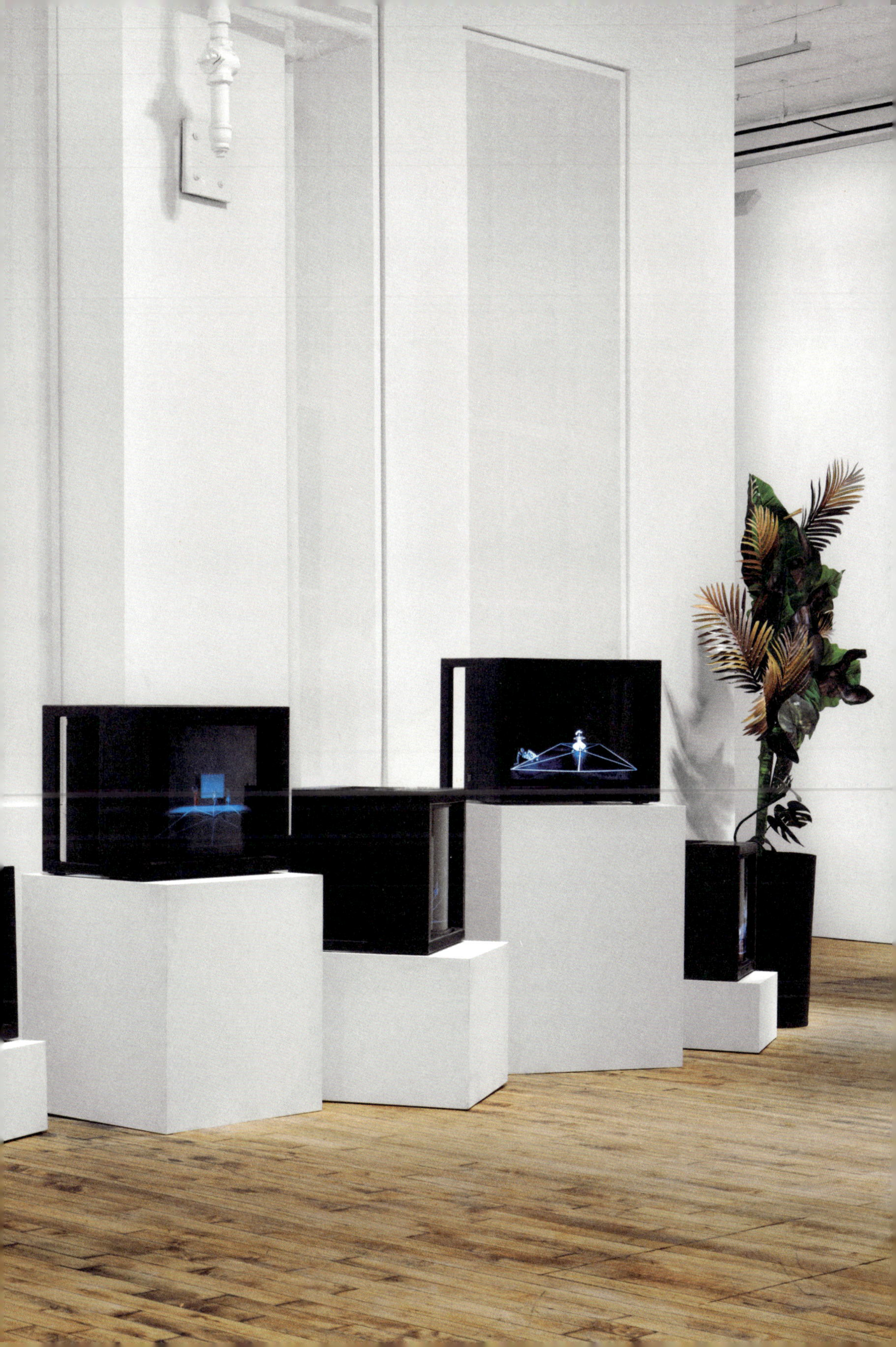

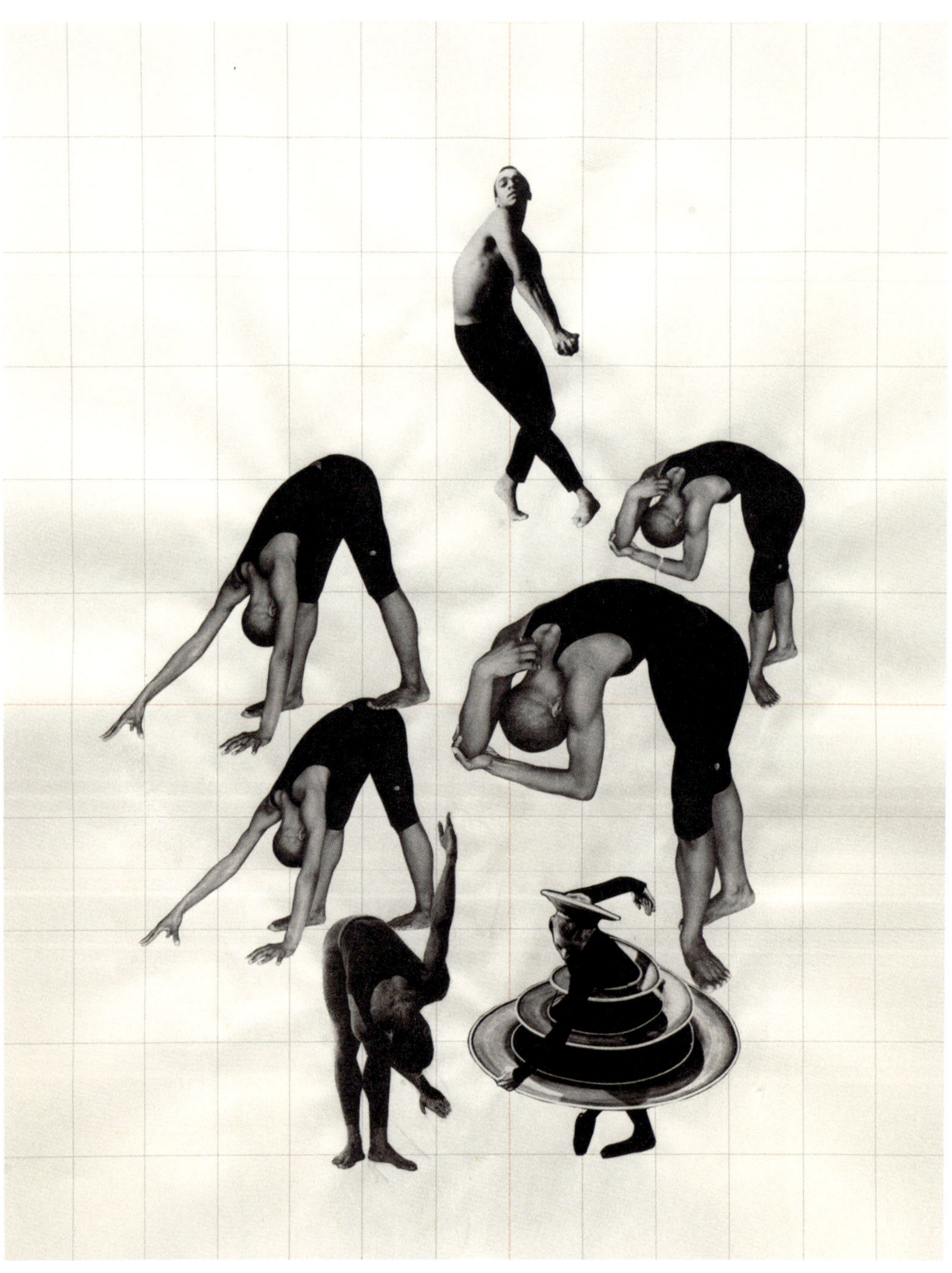

The term "theater" designates the most basic nature of the stage: make-believe, mummery,
metamorphosis. Between cult and theater lies the stage seen as a moral institution, 2021
Xerox collage on paper
66 × 52 inches | 167.6 × 132.1 cm

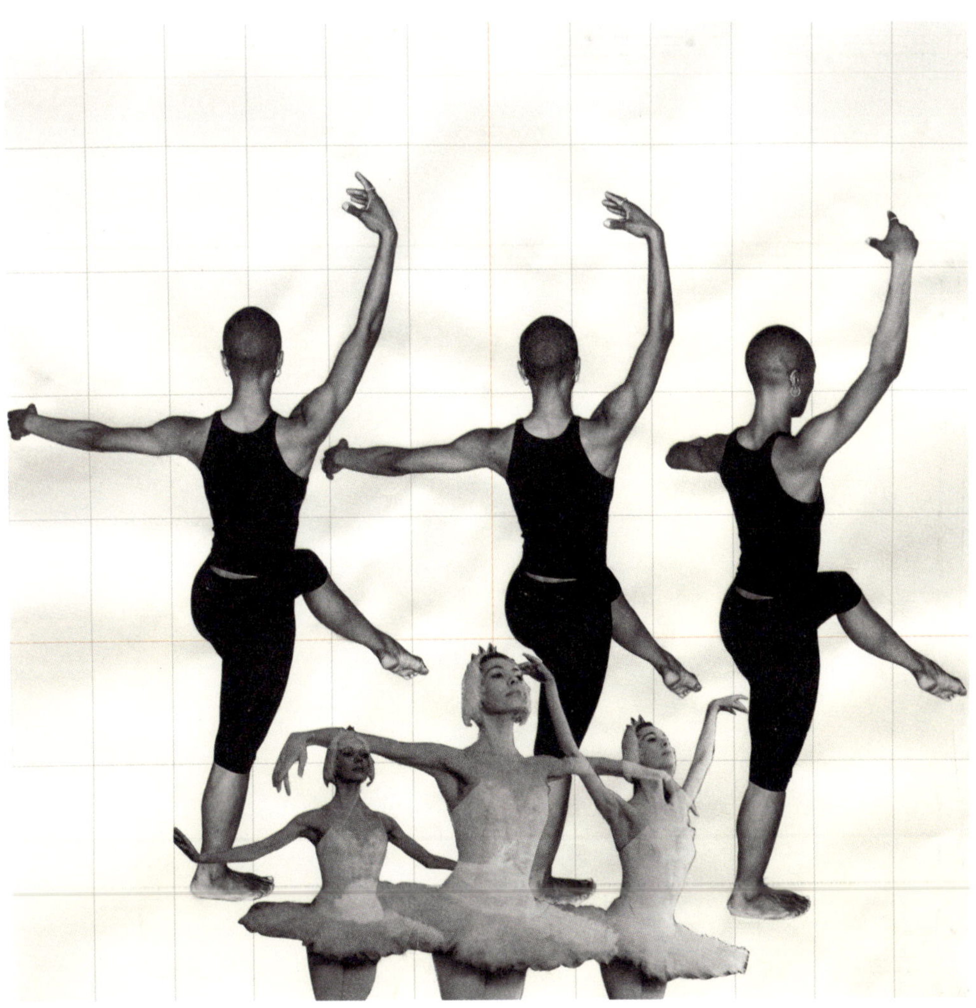

Line Intersection Sublimation: Uptown Downtown satisfactions of "Swan Lake," east west
Pavlova to Mezentseva, Madonna Whore Balanchine to Dunham, 2021
Xerox collage on paper
48 × 48 inches | 121.9 × 121.9 cm

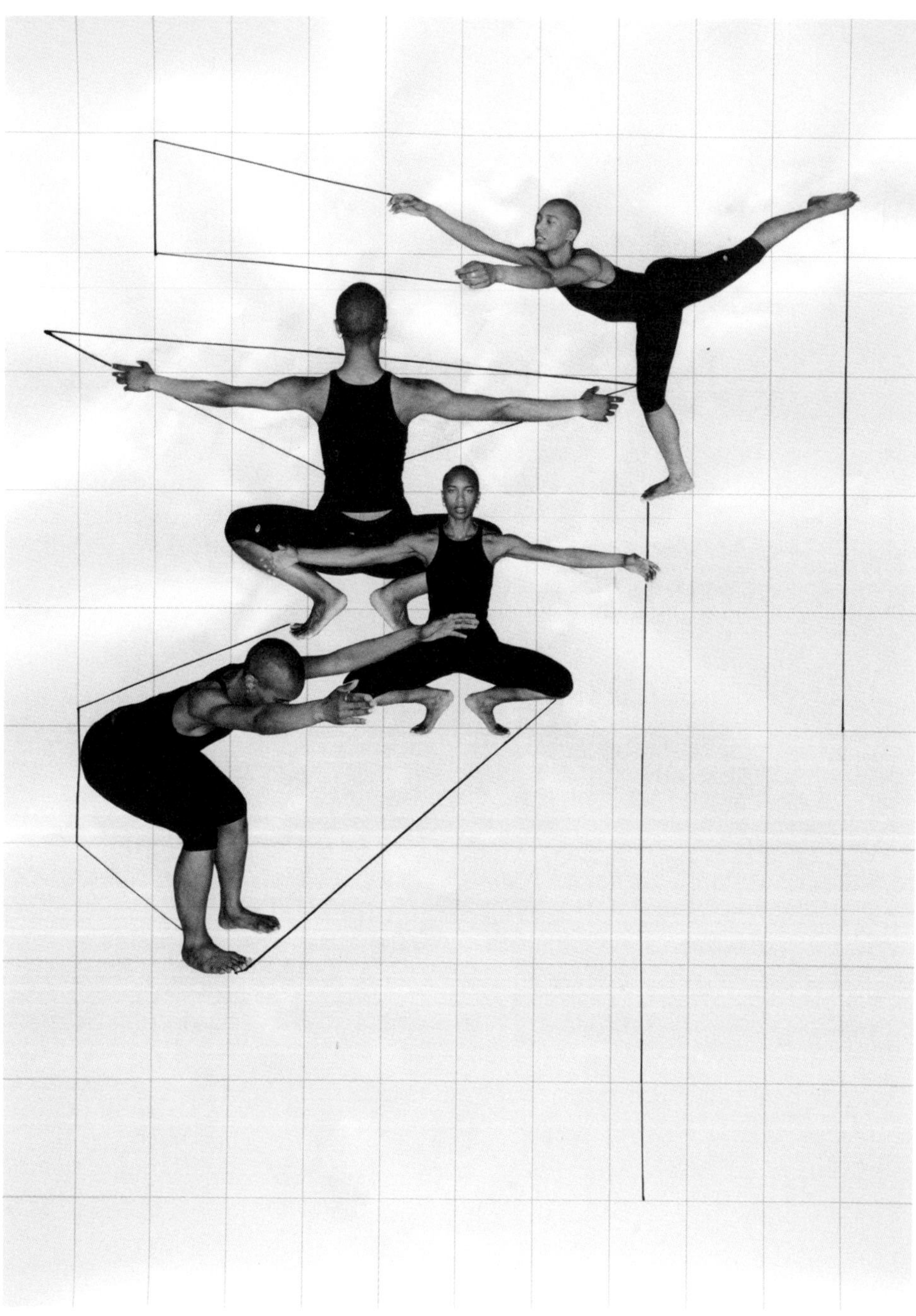

The measurement erases humanness just as it enacts it, for the deadweight signals the unfolding of modernity and collective human lives alongside, rather than prior to or after, the biological determinant is posed. Diachronic loops/deadweight tonnage/bad made measure, 2021
Xerox collage and ink on paper
66 × 48 inches | 167.6 × 121.9 cm

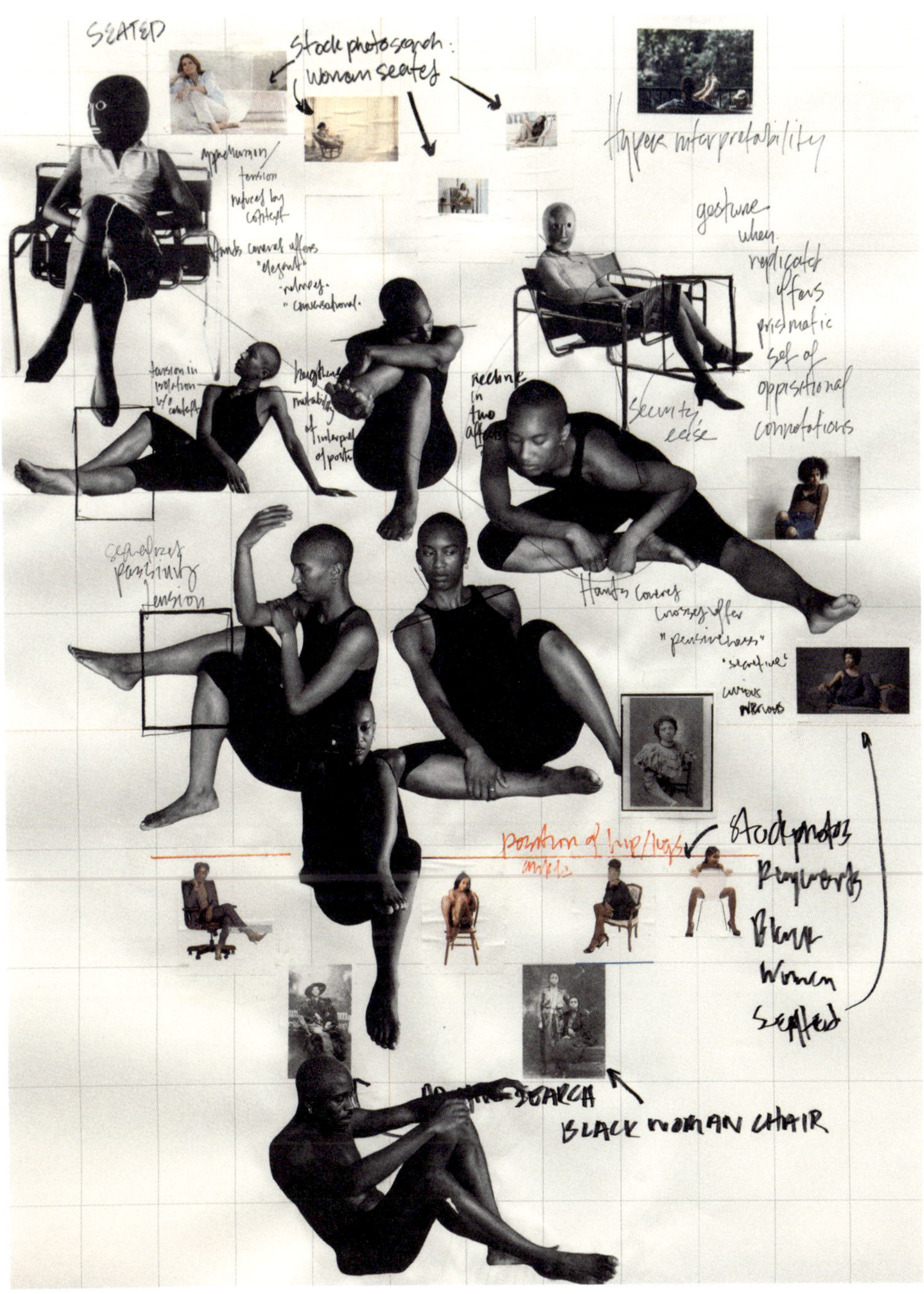

Hyper-interpretation—to be seated—figures sexualized and anonymized at rest, en largesse to stereotyping distribution, 2021
Xerox collage and ink on paper
64 × 47 5/8 inches | 162.6 × 120.1 cm

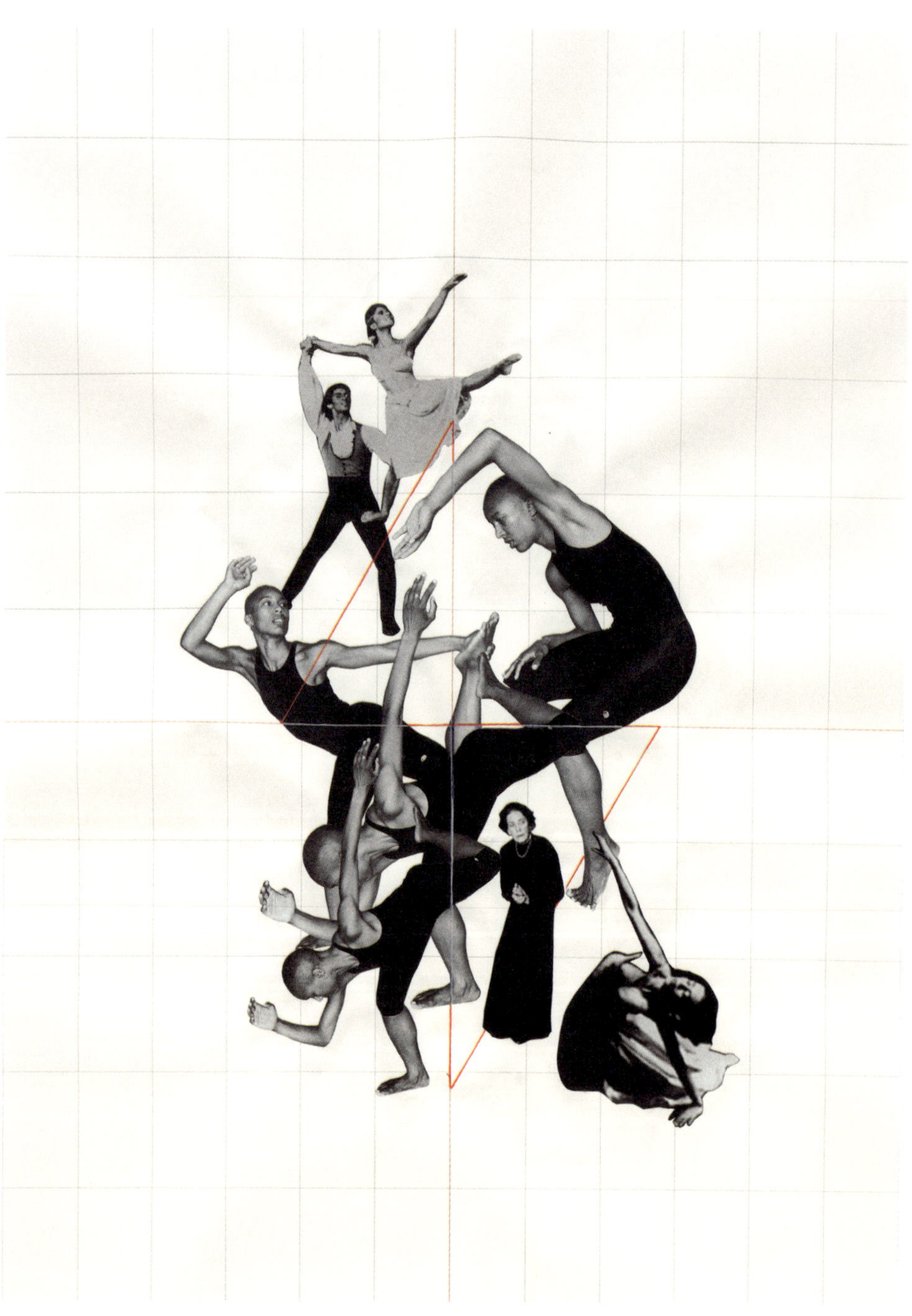

A Lift and a Kick conflated, 2021
Xerox collage and ink on paper
66 × 48 inches | 167.6 × 121.9 cm

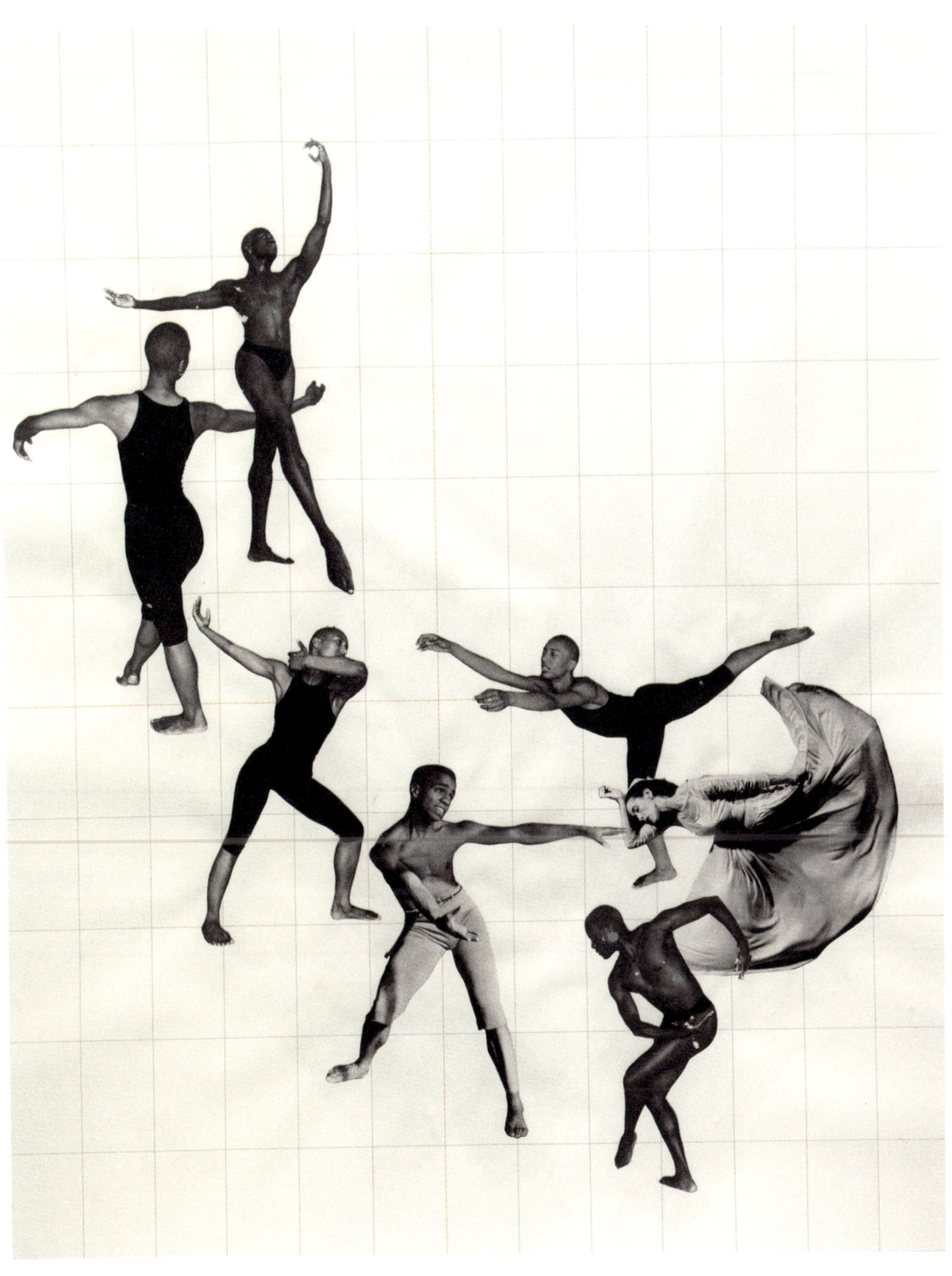

A Kick and an extension; Graham dramatic solemnity—The Lindy Hop is black dance, funerary
in solar plexus, 2021
Xerox collage on paper
66 × 52 inches | 167.6 × 132.1 cm

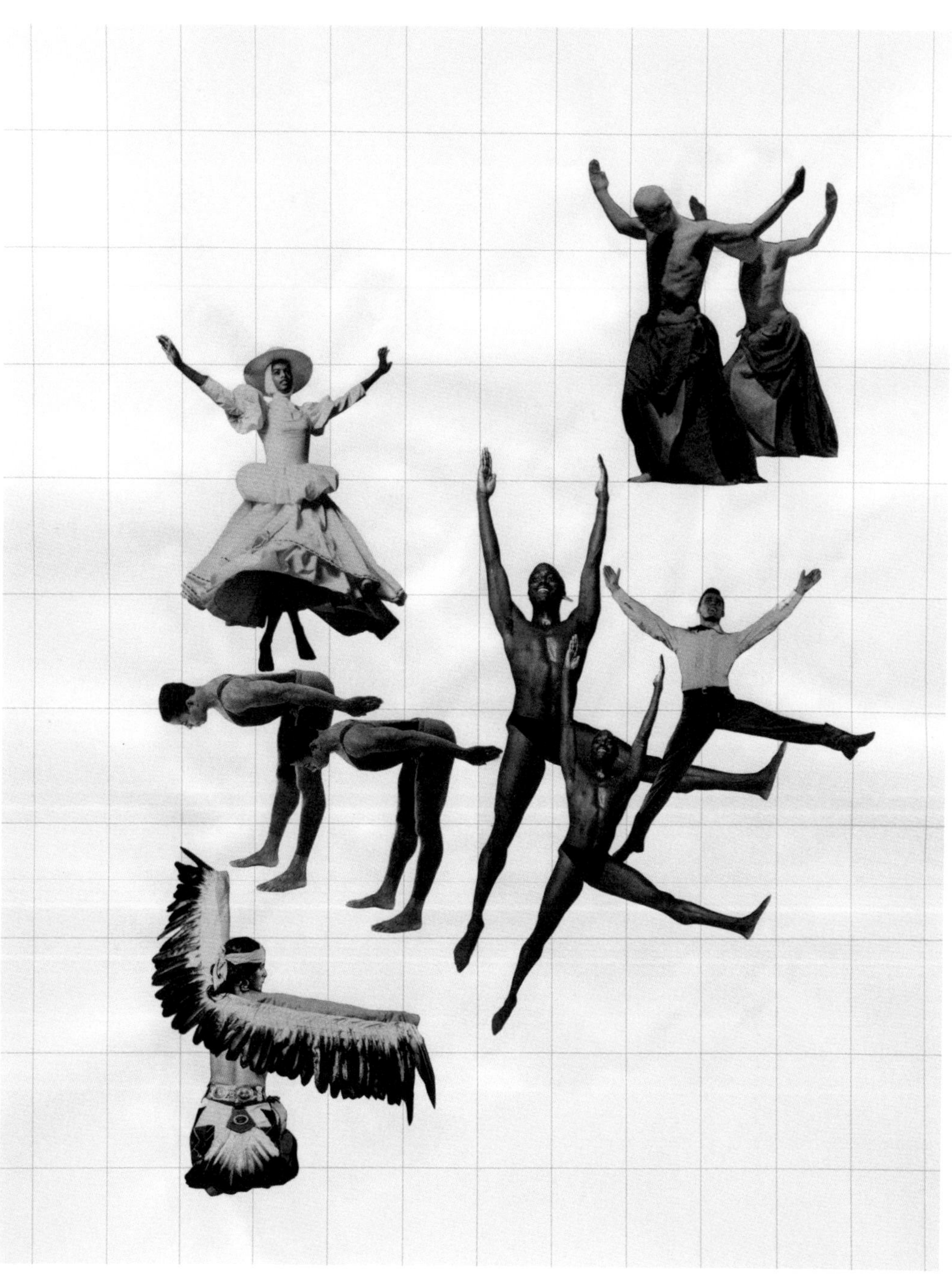

Arms outstretched—anthropomorphic Y shapes in ritual expressions turned to hyper-celebratory drama—jazz hands, 2021
Xerox collage on paper
66 × 52 inches | 167.6 × 132.1 cm

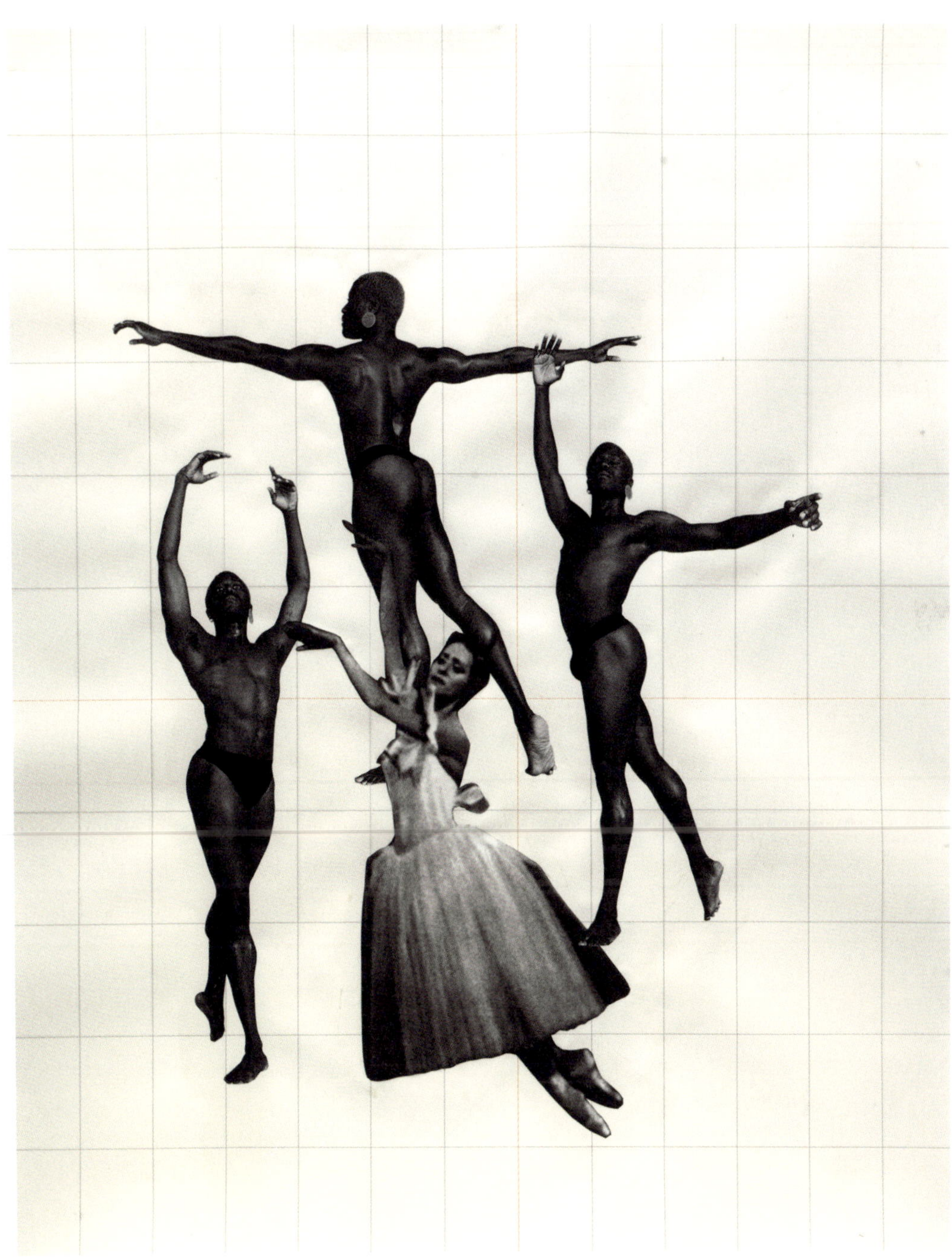

Extensions available to technique, extensions available to metaphor, extensions available through character, 2021
Xerox collage on paper
66 × 52 inches | 167.6 × 132.1 cm

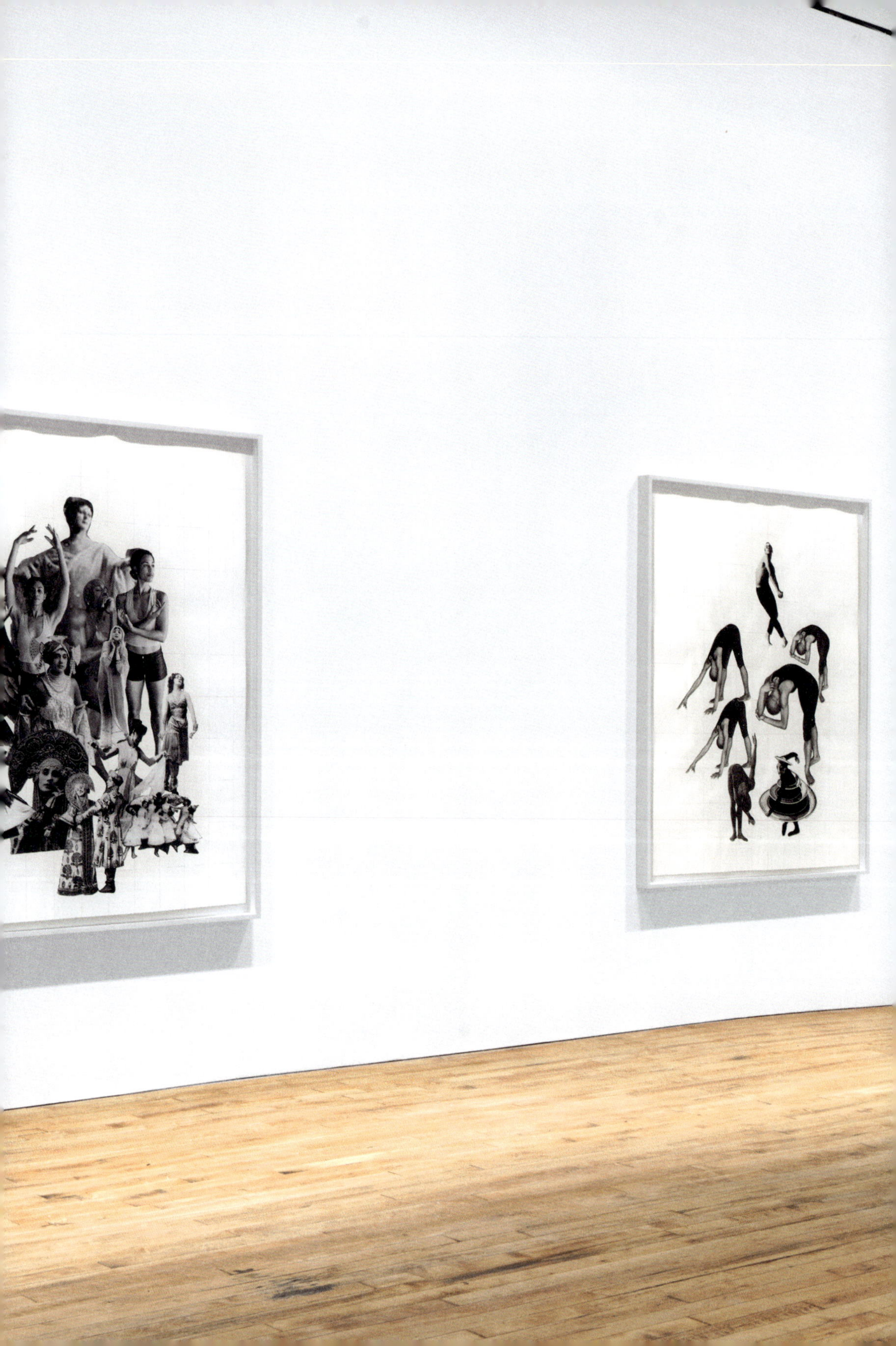

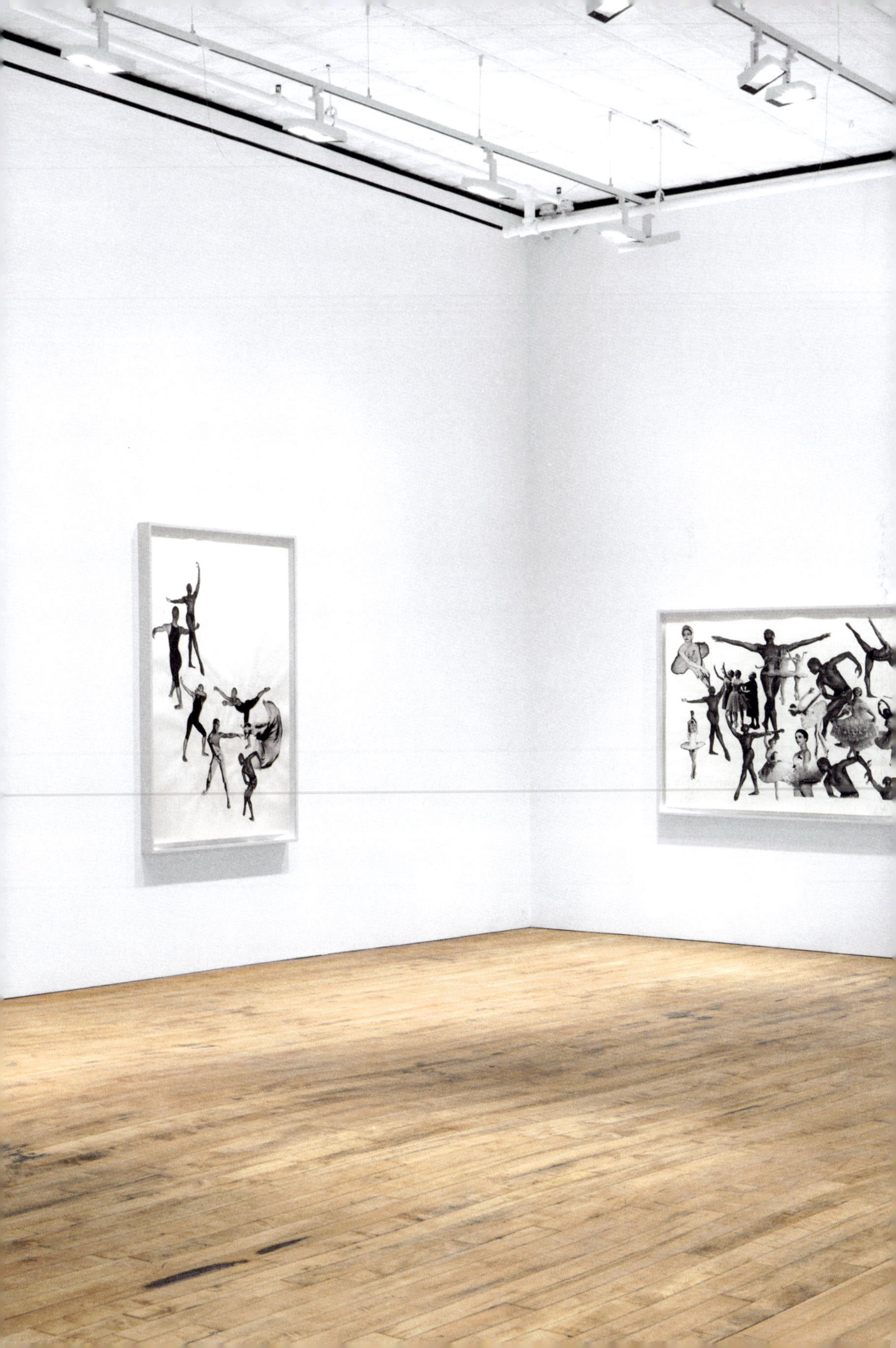

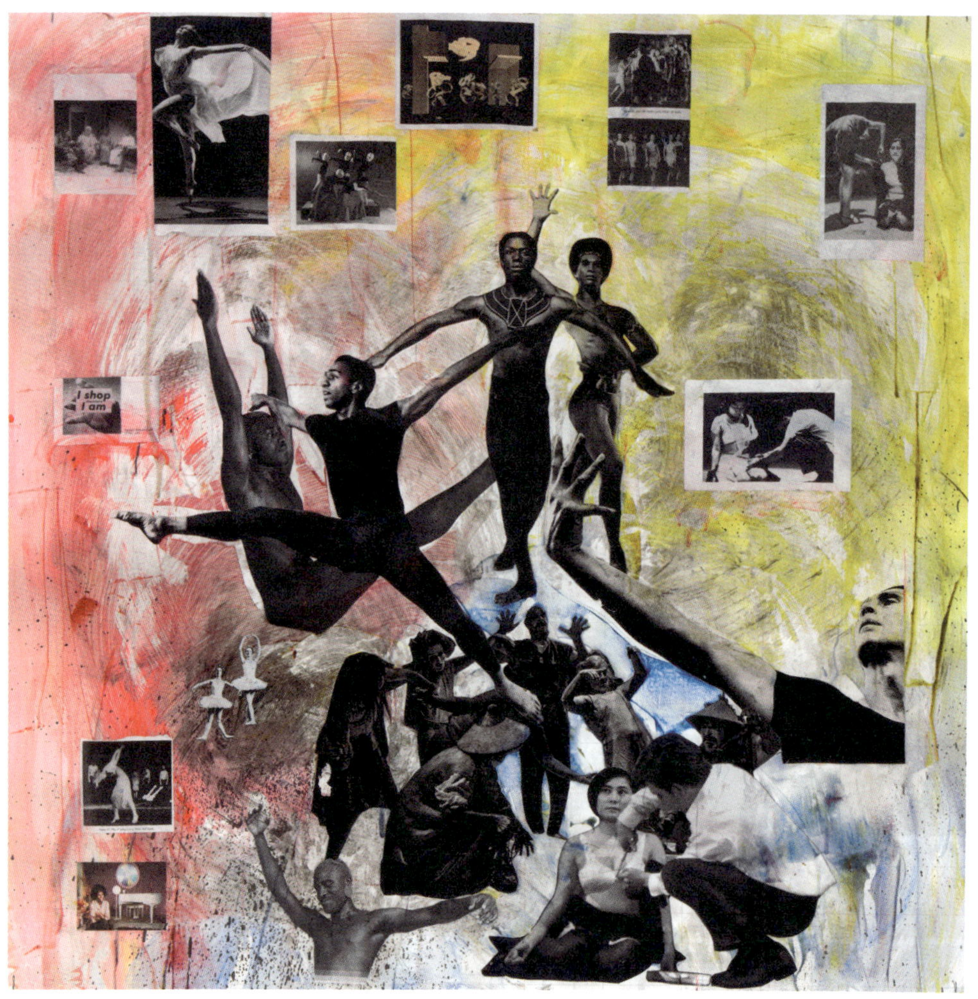

Notes for Stage, Cult, and Popular Entertainment according to place, person, genre, speech, music, and dance, 2021
Xerox collage and ink on paper
48 × 48 inches | 121.9 × 121.9 cm

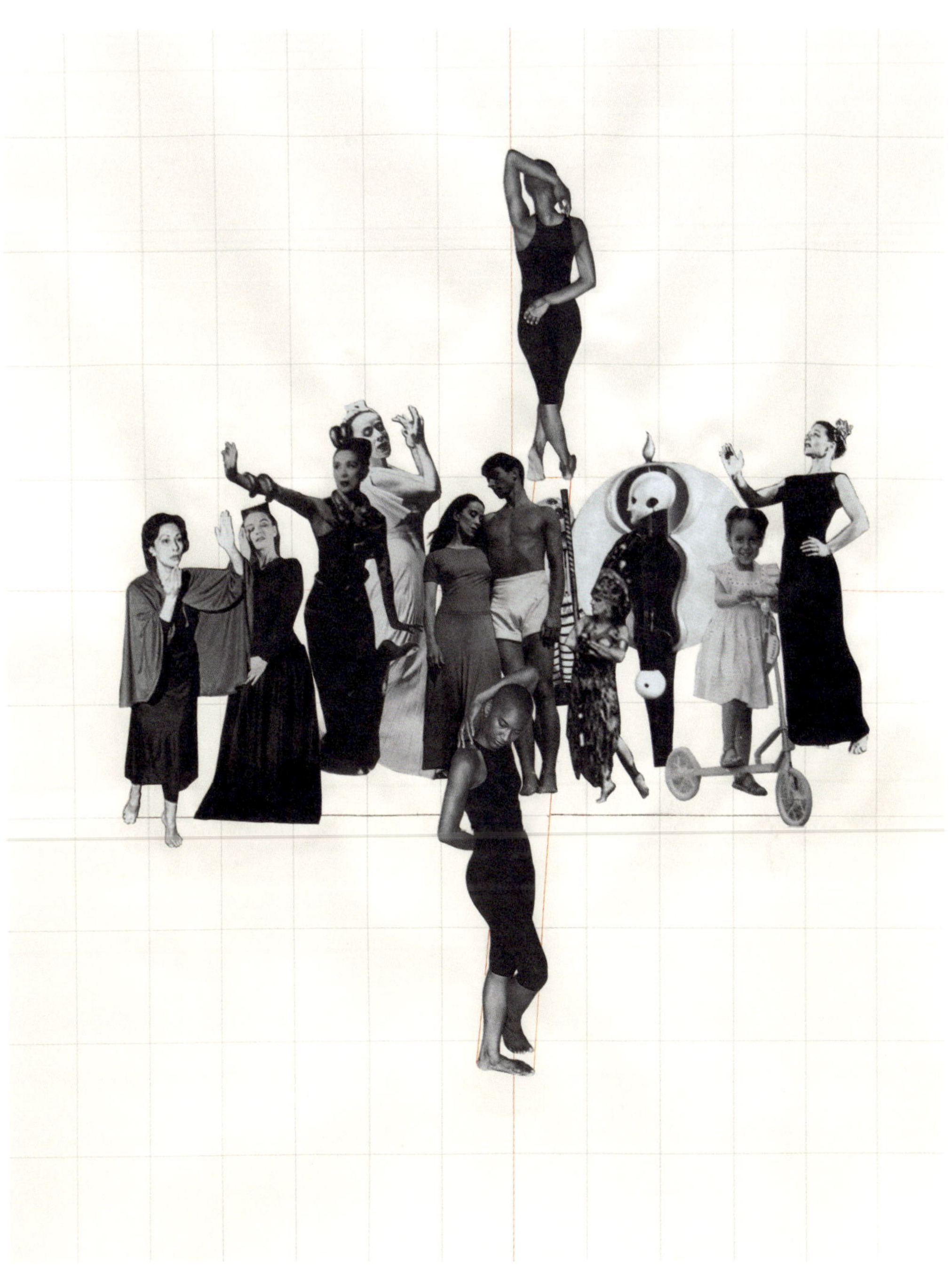

There are two sides to every Line, 2021
Xerox collage and ink on paper
66 × 52 inches | 167.6 × 132.1 cm

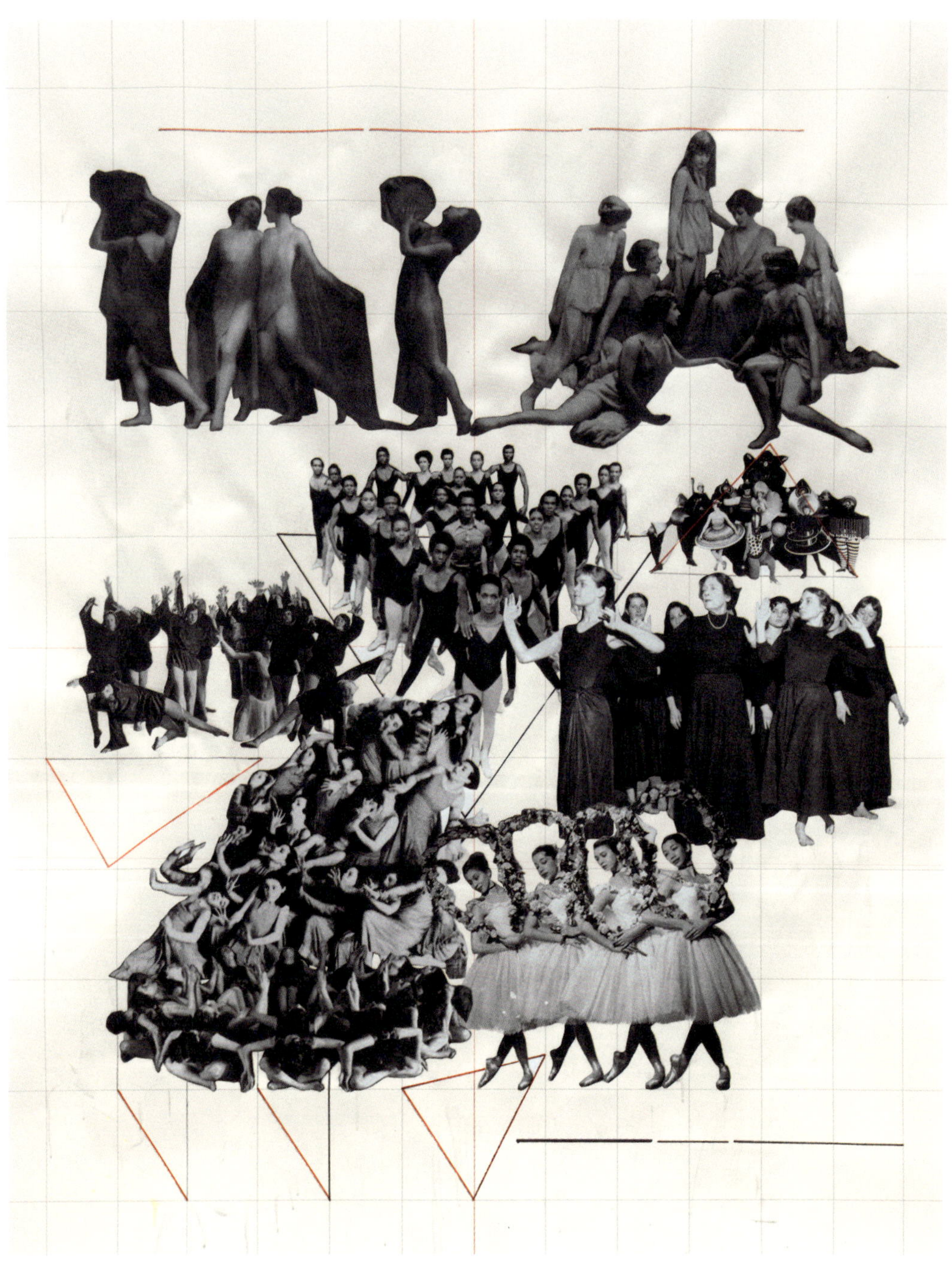

Triadic Ensemble: stacked erasures, Russes de Monte Carlo, Harlem Dance, Wigman and Duncan,
2021
Xerox collage and ink on paper
66 × 52 inches | 167.6 × 132.1 cm

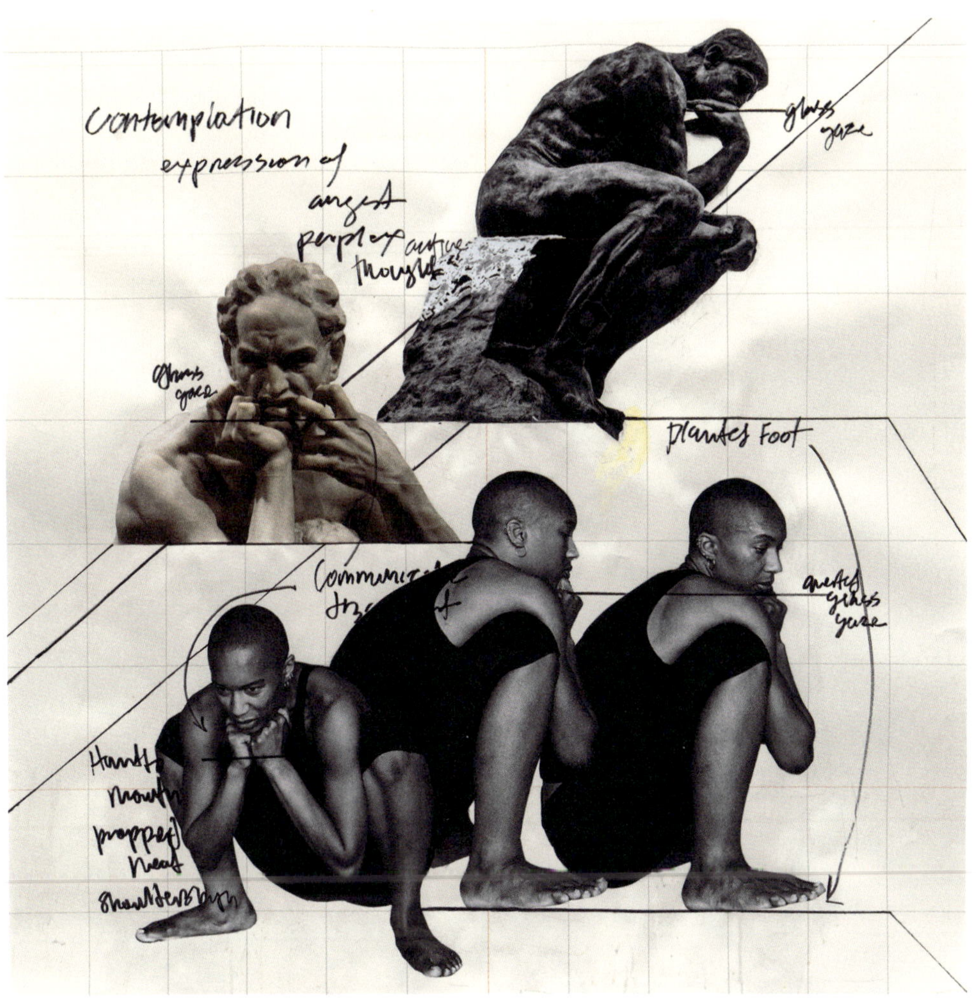

Lines of Contemplation: bitter, tense, angry, reserved, tormented (in thought) for Black and White,
marble, bronze, and flesh, 2021
Xerox collage and ink on paper
48 × 48 inches | 121.9 × 121.9 cm

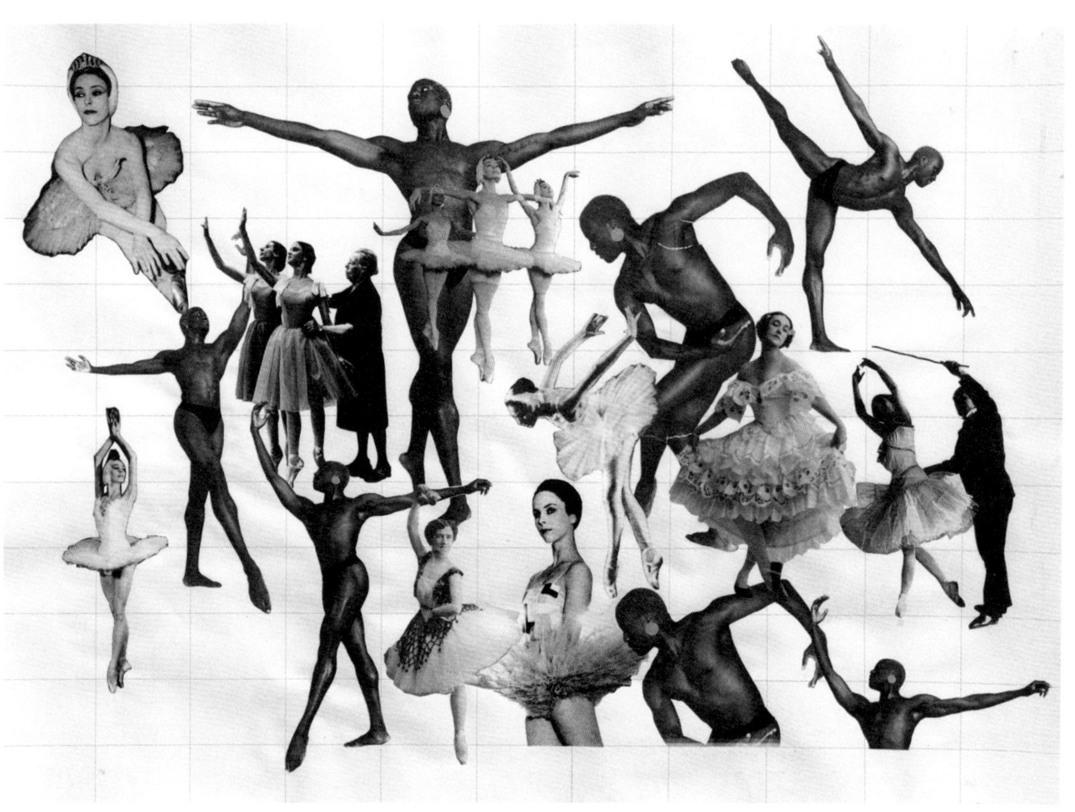

*A Line: the Diaghilev Ruler—of all the wonders that the world had to offer, only art promised
immortality, Ballet, Bazin, and de Sade*, 2021
Xerox collage on paper
48 × 65 ¾ inches | 121.9 × 167 cm

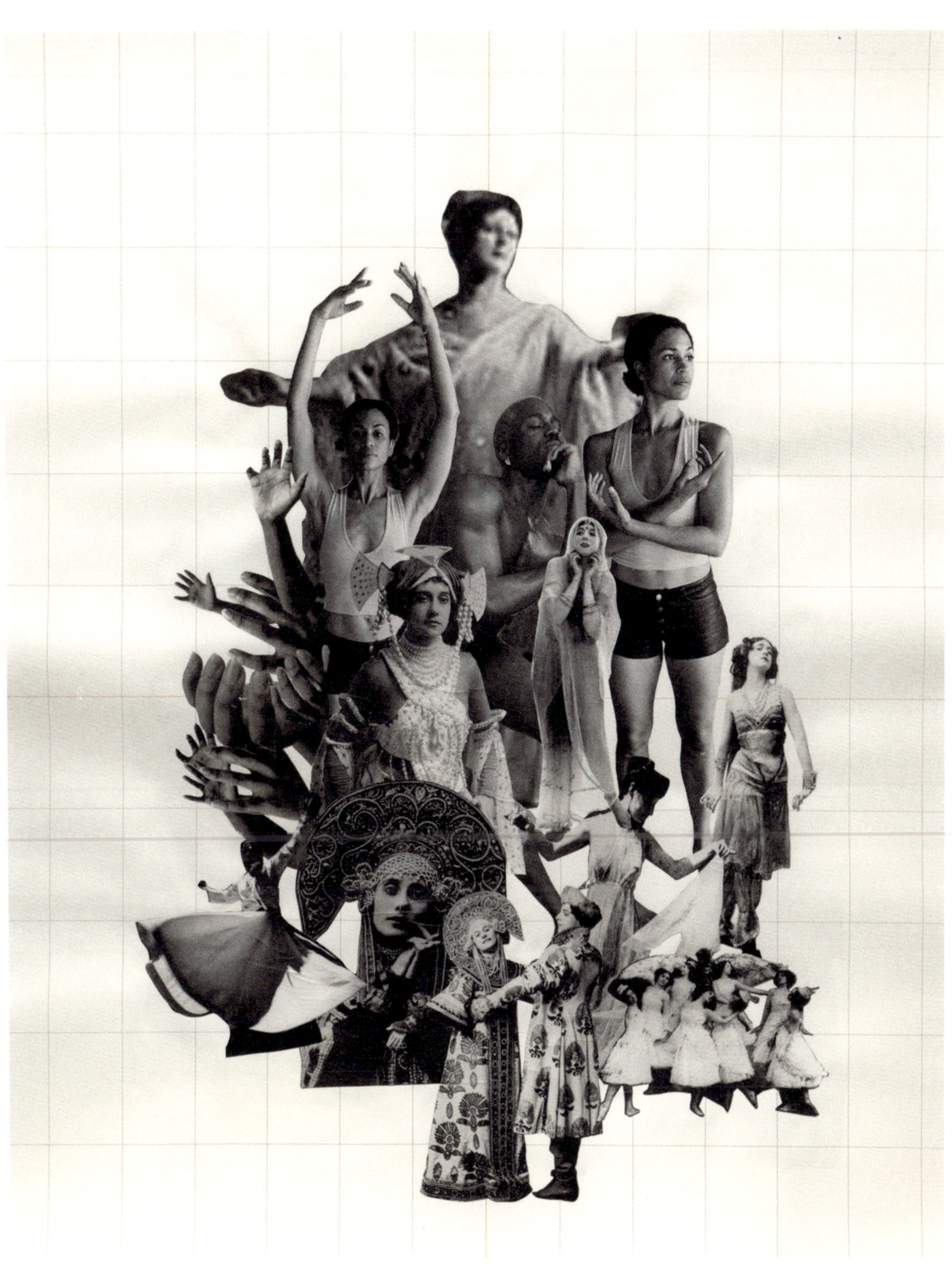

A Stack—swans, lovers, gods; costuming is the most static aspect of social order, 2021
Xerox collage on paper
66 × 52 inches | 167.6 × 132.1 cm

*Black Box, 4 points: Wading in water, Archipelago, Myth, Revelations—B. Gottschild principle—
muffled lines and ruptures—hyper-interpretation of Africanist presence(s)*, 2021
Xerox collage and ink on paper
41 ½ × 29 ½ inches | 105.4 × 74.9 cm

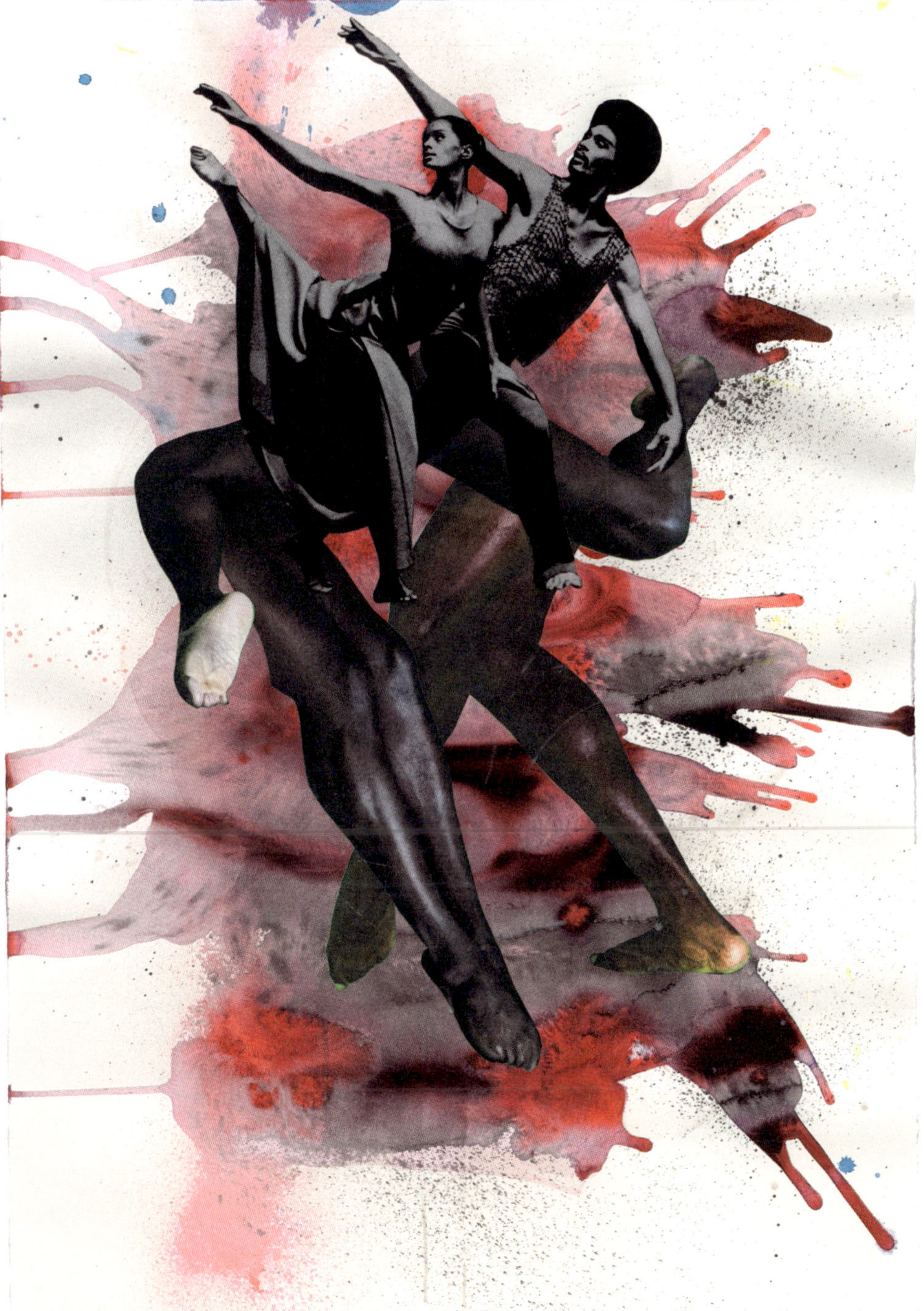

Black Box, 4 points: Ausdruckstanz and Körperkultur holds Orientalism, Primitivism, Islamophobia, and Anti-Indigenous Ideologies, 2021
Xerox collage and ink on paper
41 ½ × 29 ½ inches | 105.4 × 74.9 cm

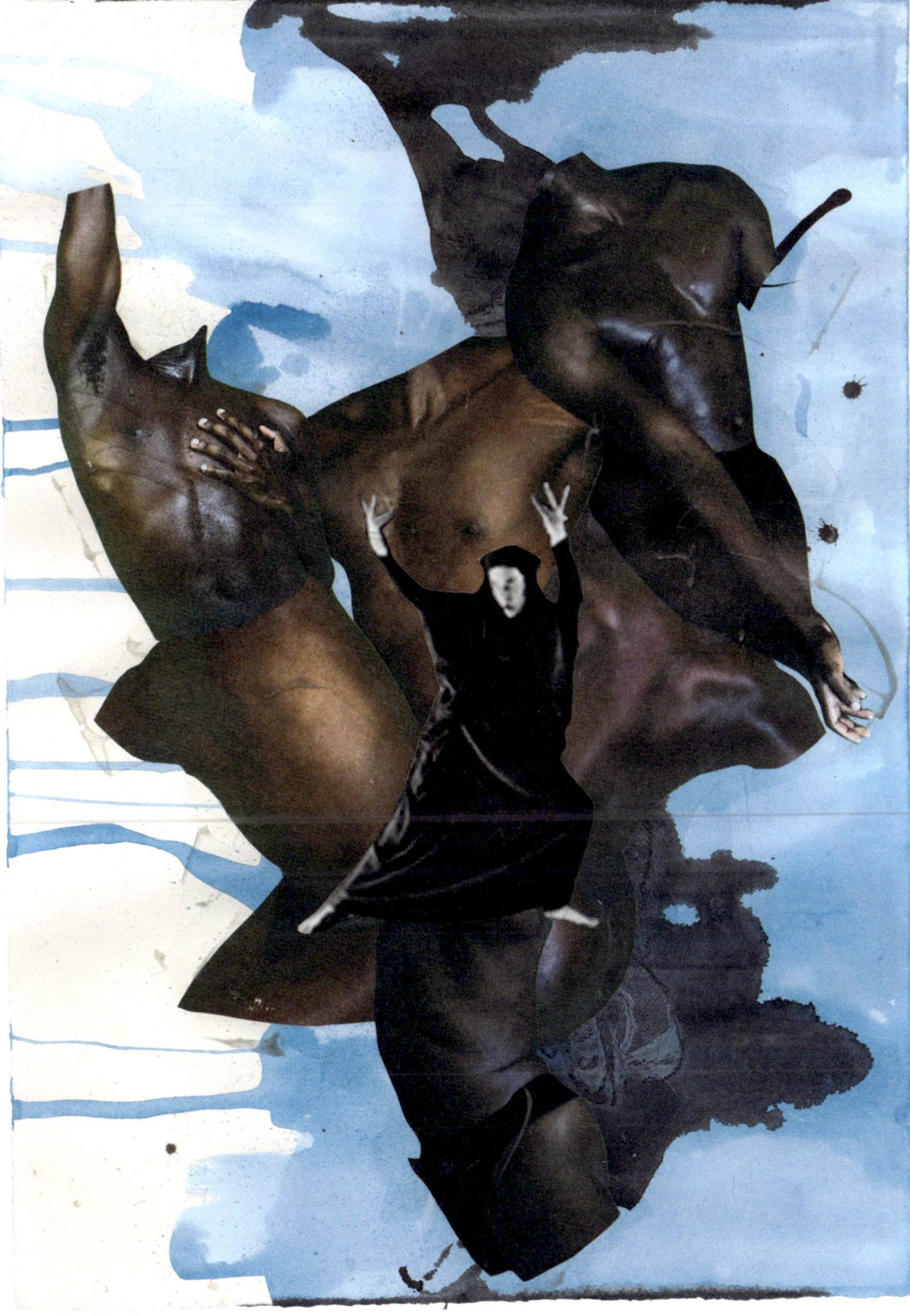

Black Box, 4 points: Horton, Ailey, McKayle contractions and expansions of drama from vernacular—arms outstretched and entangle, 2021
Xerox collage and ink on paper
41 ½ × 29 ½ inches | 105.4 × 74.9 cm

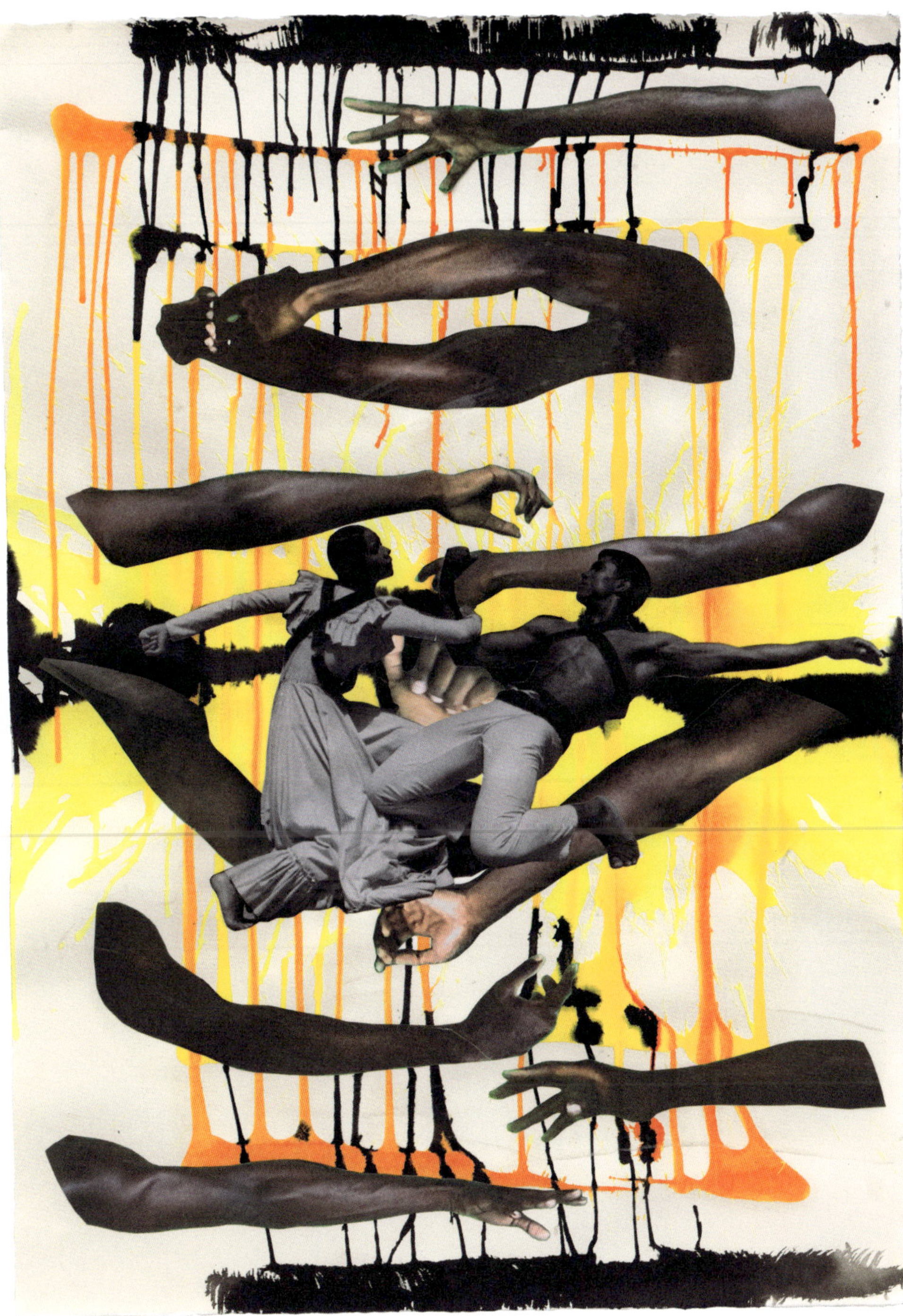

Black Box, 4 points: Greco Biblical Impulse—Clytemnestra, Eurydice, Princes, Queens, and Holofernes, 2021
Xerox collage and ink on paper
41 ½ × 29 ½ inches | 105.4 × 74.9 cm

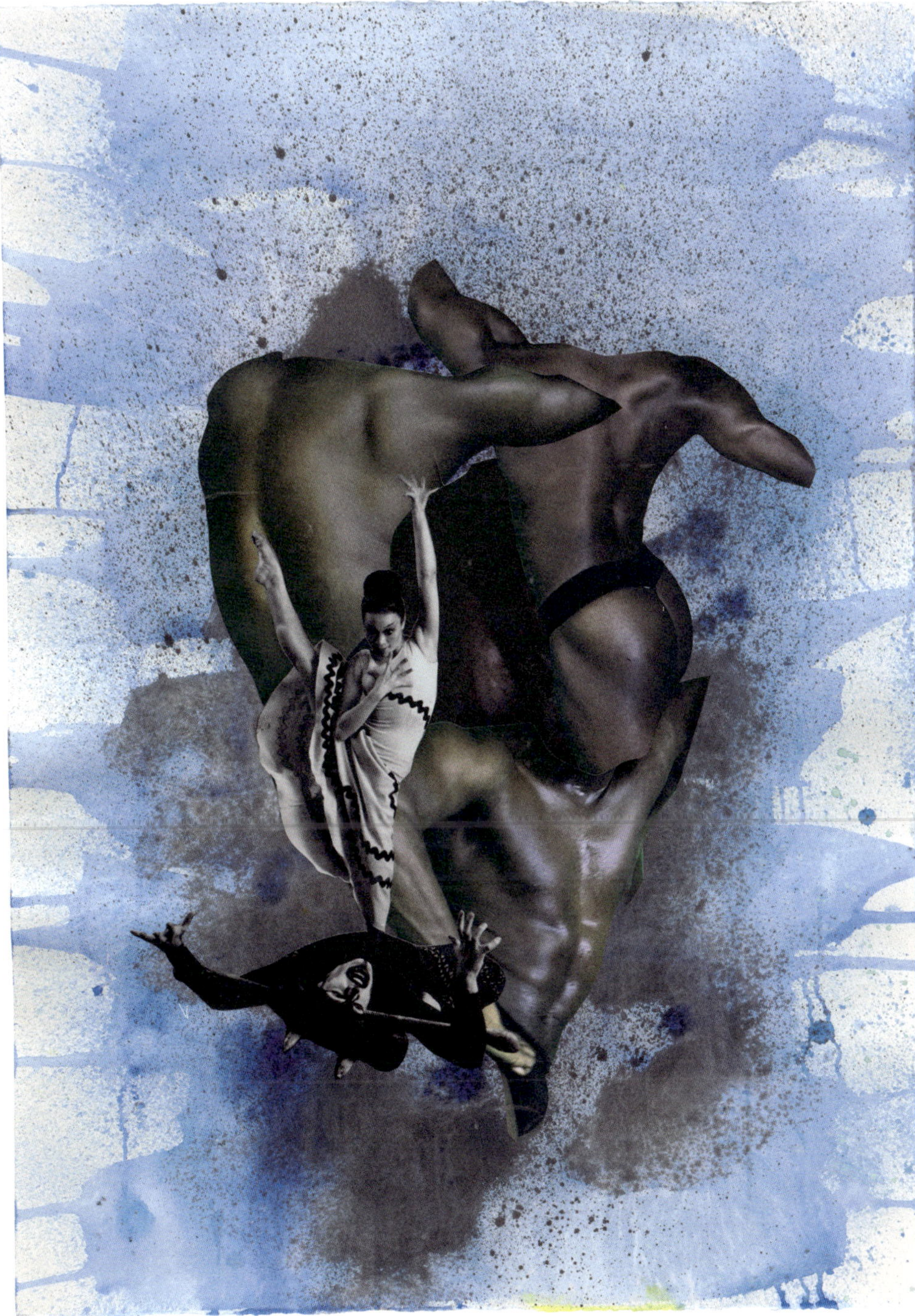

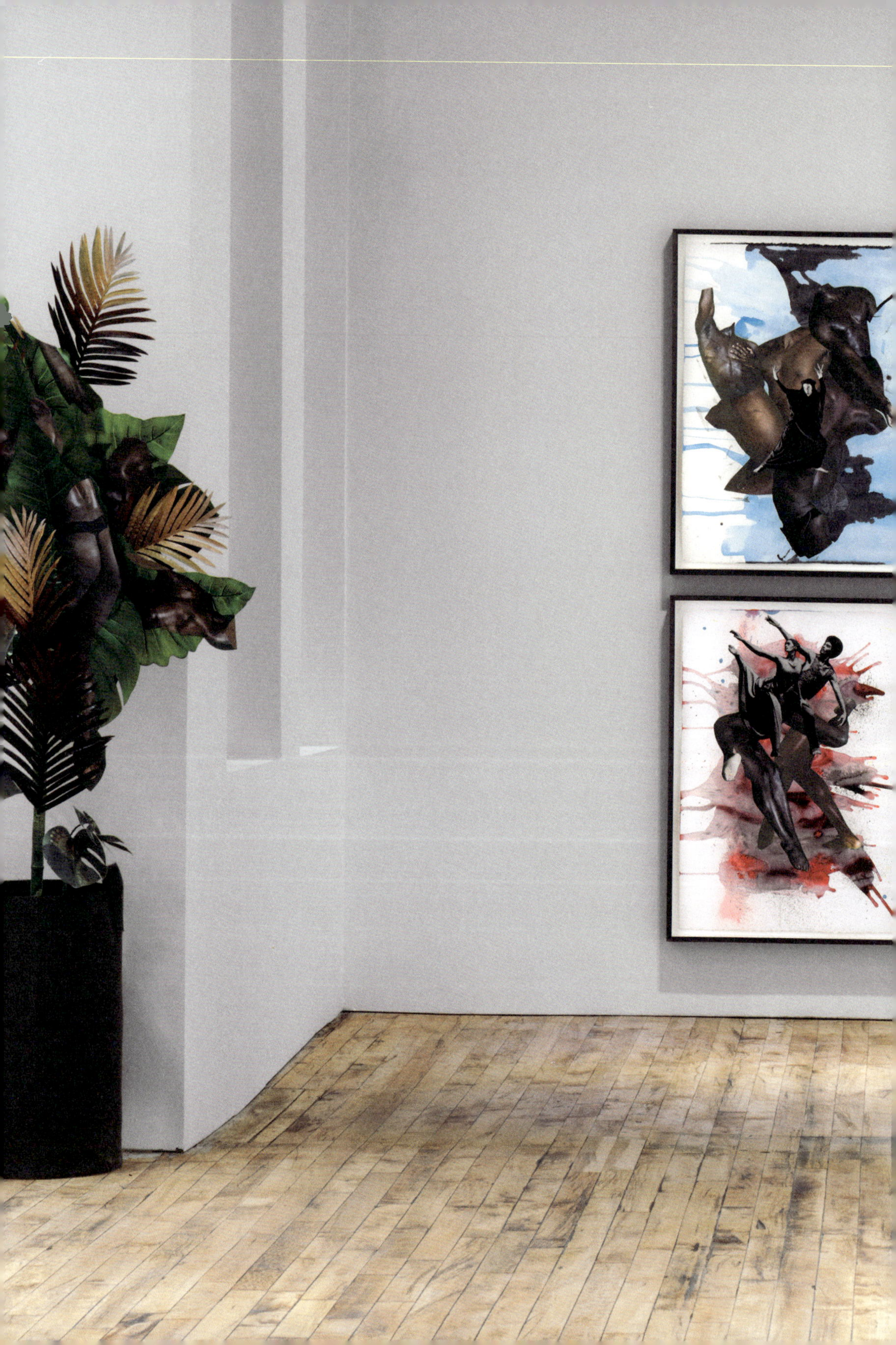

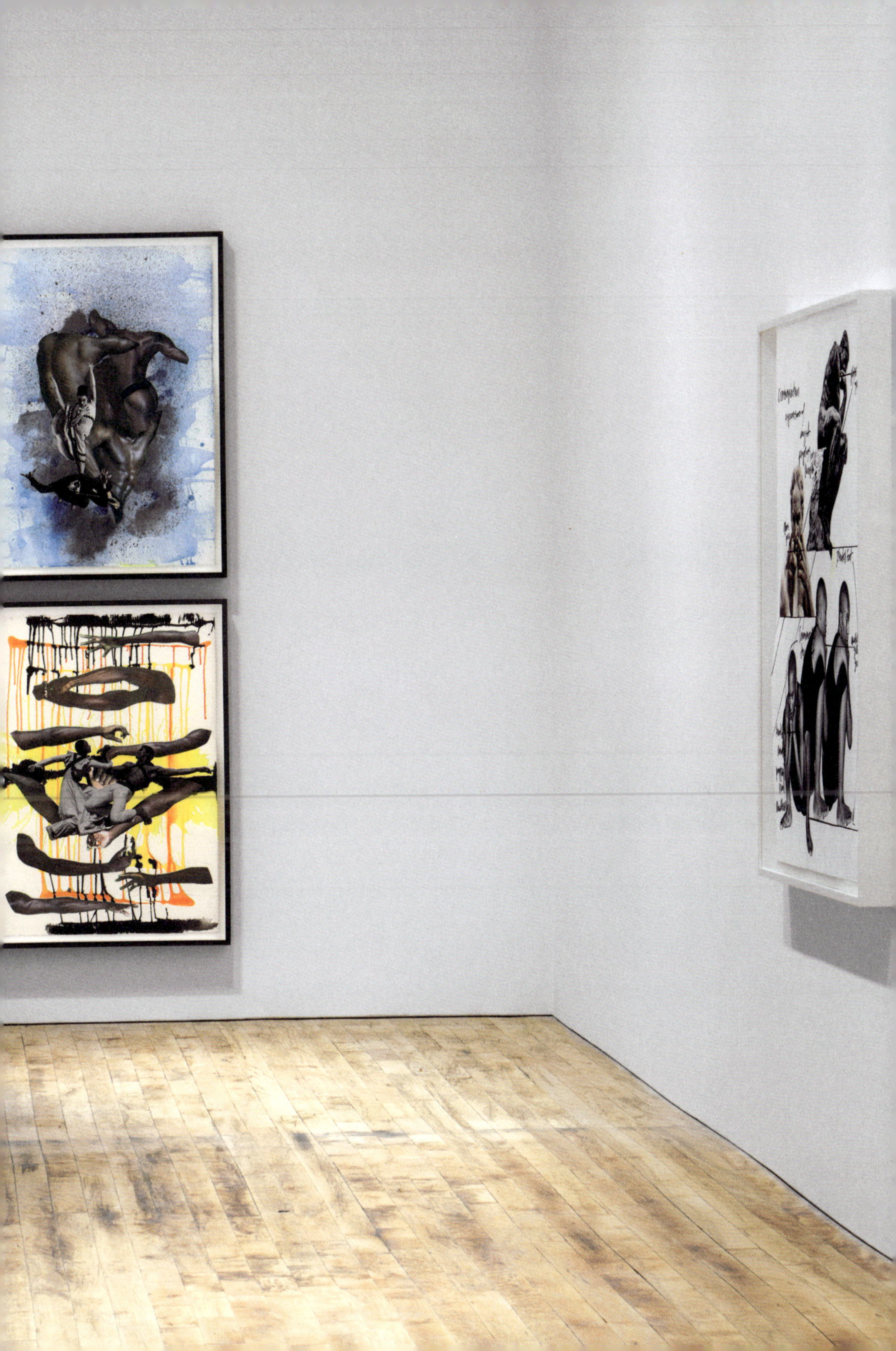

Kandis Williams and Okwui Okpokwasili in Conversation

Okwui Okpokwasili: You and I have spoken before about dance and choreography and notation—the translation of physical movement into a two-dimensional form—and this conversation is so generative, as it maps anatomy, mythology and popular culture, the black diaspora, theater, and modes of communication. I think we should start there. You were recently telling me about the American dancer Isadora Duncan's belief that dance is all from the solar plexus and nothing from below the waist. I think, too, she appears in some of your recent works on paper.

Kandis Williams: According to Isadora, it should be. She writes that anything with the hips is African jazz, and not American, and thus heathen. She was monumental in bringing dance to America. What I find fascinating is the inscription of anything related to the hips, "gyrating" or non-balletic movements, as uncivilized movements—movements that are not going to take us into the future. Movements that are not progressive. She was like, "Walt Whitman heard America singing. I see America dancing." It's all in the chest. And, yes, she does come up in some of these collages.

OO: But what is in the chest? There's lung capacity.

KW: In Western ontology, the soul. The pure soul, the clean soul.

OO: But who wants clean when it comes to dance?

KW: Isadora. That question makes me think of what whitewashing in dance looks like. Maybe this kind of cleanness is how dance was first washed for the purpose of state-funded stages, and that washing started from below the waist.

OO: At the ground. How can you dance if you aren't anchored to something? Obviously, people who may or may not be standing, or who may not be ambulatory, are dancing, but there is a sense of, at least for me, when you think about the solar plexus, that it feels sort of disconnected from an originating impulse. There are subtle shifts underfoot that send a charge up through the body, or the ground sends signals about how to move, whether you're on red earth, a sprung wood floor, concrete, in shoes, sneakers, barefoot. If you're barefoot, are you sliding over marley floors or are you burrowing your toes in wet mud? Of course the solar plexus holds information, but there is something about what your body will access, in connection to the ground; there are multiple forces, multiple trajectories. It's like multiple winds that go from the west to the east, north to south. It's a kind of spiral, a storm.

KW: An aerial. It's also nice to think about dance as having an eye and a center and various openings. Trying to build this dance notation, we can think about that east-to-west movement also as one of omissions. How could you negate the hip, for example? It feels as if it's a hectic, narcissistic concentration of some kind of omission and intention. I want to see a dance that sees all of it, sees all of it together.

OO: Or even if you can't see it, you can feel it, right? You can feel that the charge is moving through the entire body. And there is no one location. There are multiple energies in contention, always.

KW: That intention and tension is a kind of archaeology. Even seeing it as a kind of aerial from the top, there's an archaeology through the hip and into the ground and into dematerialized bodies. As black bodies, we carry so much of that funerary, so much of that axis between liveness and living, and living on and unliving, death. It's a mass of ash.

OO: Yes. And when I think of excavation, when I think of durational practices, it is to give yourself the time to start to open up the soil. To feel your feet go through the soil. To feel the pull of the hip to the ground, as if there's a chimney or smoke or a line into the stars, into the sky. In traditional Igbo cosmology, Ala/Ani is the earth goddess, and there's an understanding that your matter, your material, comes from the earth, and your chi, your spirit, comes from the sky, the past. It's as if the earth and sky meet. And we're always in the middle somehow, always in formulation, being made, and coming ever closer to that ash.

KW: In the ether. I really like the idea of wind in terms of the path creation. In thinking about a dance notation, or how to read dance, wind is such a beautiful externalizing element. I grew up as a club kid, and in the club, a smoke machine is a dancer's best friend. It mechanically masks what we may be sharing, those things that heighten space around movement, that share or perform the hazy line of sight that is the construct of the body. You can really see paths emerge or other matters being interrupted. I love plants for that reason, too. The other kinds of material that are shaping around our dematerialization and rematerialization are really exciting forms of life to reconcile with the inevitable "body."

OO: Plants are so apt here because of that constant extension—reaching toward the sun but also digging deeper, burrowing into the ground.

I like that sense of a smoke machine being your best friend as a club kid, because in some way it is about disappearing and not being seen. So then you're unleashed; you can be of that wind, you can be of that smoke, become that spiraling tendril.

KW: Ether. It meshes with the sound. Like darkness and night. They're two different forces. Nyx (the goddess of night) and Erebus (the god of darkness): I'm obsessed with their union. They have beaucoup babies.

OO: What is the distinction between darkness and night?

KW: They're two really distinct phenomena, and I like seeing them as separate entities. They have infinite implications. Their children are so varied. They have Morpheus, the Keres (female death spirits). They're violent, but they're also a tribe. Similarly, there are different kinds of dreams: good dreams, bad dreams, nightmares. Morpheus is the king of dreams. There's also Geras, which is old age and joy. Philotes is friendship.

OO: And these are all the children of night and dark. Can you talk about the mythology that drives and marks some of your notation?

KW: The indexes are thinking about the external and internal factors that build the mythic to physiological concerns and consequently the mythology that undergirds our notions of the natural, of the soul and its container, the body. Specifically, indexes of images that prepare to treat or see or erase dark bodies through narratives of positivistic lightness. I think that to be black (born conceptually through these dark phenomenon) is to be also in relation to the human whole (no aspiration ally, just in-Being), being formed, being formulated, being liminal—a matrix of being as an afterthought of seeing. Darkness and night, for me, connote space where you're without sight but not without seeing. Phenomenologically, it has, over the centuries of colonization, become to mean Being without Enlightenment, without clarity, but carrying the burdens of both. There's something nice about trying to read and write from the dark, about thinking of signage that comes without sight and the affective network that we relate to each other through. The mythic is this indexical highway that we're on all the time. So it's the preposterousness of there being one ritual without another, or one index operating independently of all others. While the "audience" gets a bad rap, we are an audience in and of ourselves because we all have the capacity to relate, to read and to write affect logics, to imbue indexes with meaning. And that gets frustrated in race and gender and nationalism. This connects to the four forks in the history of dance. The death dance of the second fork—how martial forms arose in response to how societies are organized—is almost an impediment to the first fork, which is the anthropological and social understanding of dance as it is given meaning by non-Western cultures—healing, ritual, and entertainment. The third is an appraisal of courtly dance, and the fourth is about the intellectual property of dance and contemporary movement. For me, the death dance comes out of the infinite possibilities of relation.

OO: Do you feel a need to find a discipline, or find an organizing principle that locates the death dance? Is that where the death dance comes in? Because death is also generative. Death is instructive. For me, being a black woman in this country has called for a choreographic response to what feels like an expectation of my death, or a surprise that I'm still alive. Death teaches me how to slip and evade any one idea or any one mode of relation. If the global condition of blackness or the diaspora is always contending with a particular kind of physical death, psychic death, social death, the death of history, we're constantly in a space of recovery and reconstitution.

KW: Totally. I feel that blackness is almost this communication technology for the mediation of the constant of death.

OO: Yes. The idea of reality is becoming really charged—the looseness, the shiftiness, the slipperiness of everything that we're standing on right now. We have the ground that holds us to some degree, but when the next storm comes and we're right by the river. . . . I'm thinking about storms and about how long certain structures will exist in a way that I hadn't known before.

KW: Deviation reads as instability.

OO: Especially deviation in terms of if you are having to be a black woman, a black person, in this country, to choose to work in forms that are actually formless or to eke out a path that can leave you homeless, when you could make another choice.

When you're notating dance and you're thinking about dance, you're using the spiral and death. Can you talk about that? Because I think dance notation is so strange. I like image notation because it doesn't prescribe a particular way a body has to function, but it opens up again, like a space into the spiral, into a space of potential, the liminal space.

KW: It's funny hearing you talk about this because I've seen your body move so much. There are a couple of dancers whom I've saturated my brain with over the years and whom I think about in connection to this ether. There are a few bodies that I see pulling together these texts. The text and the tension is why I thought it would be served by a system of notation. I want to be able to read these bodies together.

I guess that's a part of the practice that I'm not exactly sure about yet. It feels like the first step of citation has to be an address of the initial curiosity, but that feels fragilizing. Why give access to certain things? Especially if you're talking about a storm or death or even the idea of proprietary affective ownership. Why give someone access to your sadness? Why give someone access to your pain? Why give someone access to your body? It's impossible to move without risk in relation to something, and that is part of the importance.

But there's this other importance of shielding the bodies that helped me read many of these factors. It's giving them a space that's safe, that can be researched, that can be discursive, that can be translated into language, that can be put into pictures again—essentially, that's not vapor anymore. I work with Josh Johnson a lot, and when I see him dance, several things make more sense to me, internally and externally. It's the ritual, the background, the familial. And when I watch your body dance, a familial thing turns inside of me, and I can see more clearly.

OO: Are you talking about an archive? Are we talking about capturing something from it for an archive? Is it for you, or who is it for?

KW: I'm not sure. I think of the choreographies as traps, actually. It's like working backward from a script, working backward from a solo.

OO: What's trapped?

KW: Reproduction, maybe, mimetic production through repetition. Again, it's that aerial of the erotic, where you can see the psychic storm. It's how I'm penetrating the world. For me, it becomes a means of seeing without the need for sight, of feeling without the need for words. It's similar to the way that images can be worlds, but then also they reflect worlds—a map that clearly defines edges and omissions.

OO: And shadow spaces. That sense where everything has a reverberation, like a shadow. And shadows aren't still.

KW: And what is the shadow? Among many things, it's the darkness and night. There are many phenomena that go into making something dark that I think we neglect. Because of the racist discourse of the Enlightenment, there are so many colonial implications for why we hide from darkness.

But how does it feel for you as a dancer? Even listening to you speak now, I read you. You're a text for me.

OO: You're a text for me, too. I like being that text that's emerging in the darkness, that's not super legible. But what you can feel is the vibration and the shadow. And you can also sense the gaps and the holes. There are these sorts of spaces in between that are really charged and help to shape the shadow. I would hope that I'm something always being formed. And I would hope that there's always a question as to the shape of the word that's emerging.

KW: I mean, a question and a location. And, like you're saying, a sound. It's almost a vibration that pulls.

OO: That vibrating field is useful, and that's the space of movement or gesture that I want to work in. And so when you say that the audience gets a bad rap, it is because we have to worry about the audience if we're occupying mostly white spaces, and the audience comes with their own text, possibly over-determining, overriding what they're seeing. As black folk, people of color, we have to contend with how to make space for our own text, or how to undermine and shake up whatever text an audience comes in with. Audience is adversary. And I don't want that. I have to be grateful for some of these spaces that have invited inquiry and investigation, and the audiences that come to engage in that inquiry. And if they're coming with a particular lens and a particular way of reading, I don't mind occluding that sight, and then that becomes a part of my practice. My practice is not always a direct response to what the audience is going to do. But it's my way of keeping a liberated space for myself as a performer. I want to stay slippery and I don't want to be overdetermined. It's a generative space for me. I want to be in that space that is the forming space—that ether.

KW: That's so beautiful. It makes me think of putting words to the phenomenology of color. We actually are impactful as black people because we have this immanent color. We are vibrant. And there's a vibration. Can you imagine being white your whole life?

OO: But white people haven't been called white. They're just people.

KW: That's why they're scared. "Reality is crumbling." But it's because they just thought about whiteness for the first time. So it's as if the world is falling now that they don't have this form of order. It's a tricky dichotomy that was set up with black.

OO: Toni Morrison's *Playing in the Dark* was thinking about blackness in the white literary imagination as a projection of an abject interiority within whiteness. I guess we can get really old school and look to Joseph Conrad.

KW: And then there's all the things that are ascribed to white: virtue, purity. They're just as unformed or the act of unbecoming, a dissonance. In pre-Platonic phenomenology, Erebus and Nyx's first child is Dawn, and their second child is Aether, the god of light and heavenly ether. There's a phenomenological expectation of darkness and light, shadow and light—they're connected.

But when we start to moralize, or gender, or racialize, we create this space where the ritualistic first fork is turned into the binary of the militaristic two-way. That's another kind of line that I'm struggling with. It's a line that has two distinct sides and not an omni-direction. The straight line is the militaristic line, the edge. The space it defines will be a space of risk inherent.

OO: When I think about the militaristic line, that sharp edge, there's discipline implied. What does it mean to be disciplined? What is the charge we feel when we watch a group of disciplined people? The militaristic framework of understanding the

line is so you know what the outcome is going to be, or should be, and you see people execute that outcome. So it doesn't go beyond the thing that you imagine—

KW: It's a finality, the finality of death, or the supposed finality of it. I think that's what that militaristic line constructs—an inside and an outside. How did early societies come to militaristic dance? How were the first shields created, and why were they carved? We have so many questions about how we got here that are also issues of omission.

OO: But isn't the first shield like the arm, or your mother's body?

KW: Right, exactly. They must have come from ritual relations first, that weren't about death.

OO: But a shield is protection. I do think it might have come from death. But when you say death is not the final thing, when did we ever think of death as final? The presence of death can feel shocking, even though it's there all the time, especially during this pandemic and in the deaths of George Floyd and Breonna Taylor. The weight of the bodies, the extent of death, has been excessive this past year. In some places, though, it always has been and we've been protected from that.

KW: It's almost as if the priority of the first fork of the ritual is staging living. Ideology is pretty much the wielding of death as a proposition of finality. So much propaganda is based on the finality of evisceration. Material—flesh, the residual abstraction, the energetic imprint post-death—becomes the ether of myth. If you're excluded from a social group, you're excluded from resources, history, taken out of the infinite spiral or reduced to the ether that propels the logic of evisceration. It's interesting to think about early weaponry and genocide. There are different concepts of death. There are objects that are designed to end life without pain. It's funny talking to young black people who really want another moral praxis and want to say death is bad, but death is not bad. There are so many moral propositions that are about rebuilding ideology and not about a cognitive-phenomenological collective basis of understanding. Just thinking about the totality of a genocide, the transubstantiation of cannibalism.

OO: There is a way of eating each other that has nothing to do with consuming through the mouth. There's another kind of consumption.

KW: I think there's a kind of consumption that's predicated on race and then there's a kind of consumption that's phenomenologically so beautiful—the way we consume each other, the way we are each other.

OO: Well, then that's a kind of erotics. I mean, this is, in some ways, like the binding of souls.

KW: Healing, too. I think they say that civilization started when we started healing wounds, mending each other and staying in place. Was the first death sad?

OO: So death is not necessarily bad. You talk about some of the children of Nyx and Erebus.

KW: Geras is really beautiful. Geras is born old and just keeps getting older. They have a kind of minor wisdom. Temperance is one of their children. Patience.

OO: But those virtues are always so problematic, right? Purity, especially.

KW: Basically. They all have their sibling bonds. Thinking about Dawn and Aether, schooling Morpheus and the violent deaths on how to be nice to Joy and Old Age or something. It makes me less scared of death. Thinking about Hypnos (Sleep) and Thanatos (Death). They share one wife and she's the goddess of hallucination, meditation, and relaxation. So that somewhere in between understanding, death and sleep are synonymous. You get to that liminal, really beautiful place of dreams, meditation, hallucination, visions.

OO: And how does this all manifest in the body, when you're working with performers or dancers? What is the space that you make? And how do you make space to even start to trace or enact these lines? Do you go back to the mythos or do you go back to the origins?

KW: I'm obsessed with origins but that doesn't mean I think they really exist or they're necessary or meaningful. I love the idea of it, and I think that's the line, too. It's almost as if it's an imagination of an origin, a future, a movement around space. But it depends on the text, or on the dancing.

OO: The dancers are the text for you. You're reading it. When I was looking at the performer in one of your pieces who was enacting Tatsumi Hijikata's girl—

KW: Lina Venegas, my big sister. She was the first person cast for a work I made in Vienna. When we met, I was really vulnerable, and I have a tendency to produce texts as weapons when I need to. That's something Hamza Walker and I talk about a lot—how to weaponize your accumulation. Cauleen Smith said once that "black artists are accumulation machines"; we have to be because we lose so much in the overdetermination of other people's scripts. What kind of accumulator are you becomes a question. And I accumulate shields. And Lina saw my shield.

Lina is a very petite woman of color who has been dancing in Vienna for seventeen years. She said, "I'm literally in a world of white giants." In the performance, one of the first things she did was put her hands in her mouth and pulled her mouth open. That became the first place of work for us as writers together. Where do we want to see how people are looking at us and where do we need to see just what's happening inside? How do we need to feel what's happening inside? It's somewhere in between Hijikata and Hex Intense for me. The legibility. The total artwork. The existential crisis. It's as if it's a geometry that is compellingly diasporic in internalizations and externalizations, gasps and exhales and last breaths and first cries. Questlove wrote a four-part essay on what "cool" is and what black people have done for "cool."

OO: What have black people done for cool?

KW: His essay is called "When the People Cheer: How Hip-Hop Failed Black America," aptly published by Vulture. Questlove makes a thesis around, essentially, how "cool" acts as a social order and as a currency that we rarely get to keep as a community, one that excites and intimidates non-black people. Norman Mailer invented the term "hipster" in the essay "The White Negro." He writes about the modern world and its devaluation of life; that whites of his generation must face a kind of mortality of their own making. He speaks of existential dread fueled by witnessing the Holocaust, then the nuclear bomb, and, as he writes it in 1957, the conflict in Vietnam is being ceded. To cope or manage these realizations, he, sadly, looks to the eviscerated black male body, the discourse of cool is born. The actual quote is: "So there was a new breed of adventurers, urban adventurers who drifted out at night looking for action with a black man's code to fit their facts. The hipster had absorbed the existentialist synapses of the Negro, and for practical purposes could be considered a white Negro. To be an existentialist, one must be able to feel oneself—one must know one's desires, one's rages, one's anguish, one must be aware of the character of one's frustration and know what would satisfy it."

OO: Do you know, when in fact, I think it's the reverse, dear? I feel like what the Negro has been able to do, or black people, we've been able to inhabit your synapses and work our way around it.

KW: Josh's cool moves things. Josh moves people. He was an Ailey dancer and a Forsythe dancer. You can see Josh as trend itself. You can really see people's desire to give power to that line. They bow to it, they supplicate to it. But it's terrifying in some ways, too, because people want to wear it, they want to be it.

OO: Another kind of consumption. He's not destroyed by it, though?

KW: I think he's destroyed a little bit by it every time. The first time we did *Affect: Network: Territory* was right after Philando Castile was murdered. I'm thinking about that script, that death script, the discipline that Philando Castile's girlfriend is implying, in that moment—I was like, Okay, this is called training.

OO: While your lover is bleeding out and your child is in the back and you have the presence of mind to make sure that you videotape this so that it can be seen and witnessed. That's some navigation. That's discipline.

KW: It shook me hard. I couldn't watch it. And her also holding the phone.

OO: And the multiple audiences that she was addressing; both the police officer who still would not put his gun down and the prospective possible audience.

KW: The audience then is inherently the site of caricature. Caricature is turned upside down with a cell phone, self-profiling as a form of participation. From all those videos, we understand that there is a space where the audience is our only protection, as Hartman alludes, the dead archive. That exhibition/stage/profiling/cognitive order becomes our only safety. Where the caricature and the thing, the line, that makes us legible become the only tether to being otherwise eviscerated. And that becomes such an important tether, communication-wise, acts as wisdom. It becomes such a dominant language; that we all learn these scripts without learning them. We're reading them in the dark. And we're performing them pitch-perfect, in very critical moments of crisis. I have thirteen younger brothers and sisters. There's a lot of fear for the black male body that's just inherent. Having a body that, I think, is insanely gendered and insanely ungendered, constantly. *Affect: Network: Territory* starts in the dark. Josh starts dancing, which is already this beautiful draw, because he's like wind.

People feel him moving around even if they can't see him, and he's deft and he can stop. The balletic and the Butoh are the alien forces that are swirling. So it's got a gospel energy. He's got an order with his presence. Then I planted one person to turn on a cell phone flash in the dark, and by the end of the performance, everyone's done it. That one person turns into a crowd of people with the desire to see, to capture, to record. And seeing the audience slowly become aware that they're chasing him is a part of working with Josh. And that becomes the trap, an invisible trap, a tether.

OO: The audience doesn't move, right?

KW: Actually, they move wherever we take them. I think I could get people to go off a ledge with the right libidinal combinations. They've gone down streets, up stairs, into rooms, into corners. That's almost the trick or not the trick, but the trap with Josh is how far will they go to capture and witness this body falling, rising. We start a lot of the performances with his face down and a lot of the blocking is denying the audience his face. And it causes a fervor that's palpable. If he starts face down and moves as slowly as he wants, it just builds. Whereas when I work with white femme bodies, for instance, people don't want anyone else to know how much they know those bodies, how much they look at them in private and defer to them in public. They look away. The synaptic stage gives out to desire and discourse. As bodies, their symbolic register is open to counterfeits so the audience is uniquely self-aware. I imagine this is also due to four or five decades now of white feminist discourse that has stretched from archetypes of man-eating vagina dentata to bimbo/muse worship, in no less than four generational waves, all tied to the inheritance of wealth procured by a violent white masculinity, another libidinal bounty. A white femme body in exposition or exhibition begs moral questions, the synaptic why is that happening to her?

OO: I loved when you talked about writing the text together. That you and Josh and you and Lina are writing particular texts under certain conditions, under the conditions of your meeting and the particular places where you happen to be, the geographies that you find yourself in and coming from. But what is it about? How do you mark how you're moving through these texts?

KW: I think that's why I have to do the notations, so I can do that without hurting myself. I love working like this, and I do love writing together, but it is painful. I feel like this is the thing with the dancer's body. I feel removed from that system of training, how we detach it from social scripts. Going through that kind of body education feels so far from what I'm able to tolerate as a human, yet I admire the use of technique, even if the cost of the training is the obscurity of certain metaphorical extensions of the "human" being. Dance and Theater give access to the means and modes of internalization and expression of character. It becomes painful to meet someone and explore questions such as, How are you trapped? Where are you burdened? What does it feel like? What face does it have? Can I make a costume for it? Should it be a puppet? Where's the smoke machine?

OO: But that's not what you do.

KW: That's kind of what I do.

OO: Right. So are you notating all of this? What are you bringing in? This is how you're not hurting yourself.

KW: If I have a terminology, which I am guessing at with the notation, I feel like the work can proceed me.

OO: No. If notation is a kind of anchoring, something that anchors you to life, to living, or if it helps you look at pain from a distance or use a sculptural notation as a sculptural space—I think dance is that.

KW: Inherently.

OO: But it's both inside and outside. There has to be some kind of ecstasy in the release, a resistance to standing in one place. There's a freedom and an ecstasy. And yes, be able to excavate and go into the dirt, but also be emerging as well and have the wind carry you. It's movement. And dance is a strange thing because it comes with various meanings and vocabularies or connotations.

KW: What about courtly dance? Dance made to please the aristocracy, for the eye of the king. How does it feel to dance on the stage? And how does it feel for you to dance off the stage? Where is the stage in your performances, and is that one-directional?

OO: Courtly is about the stage. Sometimes when I think about courtly, I think about another kind of relationship, an agreement, a kind of ballet. But the stage is about display, if courtly is about displaying a particular position or readiness or openness. Sometimes you have to consider the stage in terms of how people are in relationship to it. Again, it's the audience looking at each other as much as looking at you. And so your body isn't the only one at stake. I think that there's always a question of how we position the people who aren't obviously performing to recognize or feel their own place in relationship not just to the performers but to each other. In particular pieces, I often start before the beginning. The audience comes in at a certain point, but I've already begun because there's a current that I want to charge beforehand. In the interest of blurring or softening the lines, making more gaps, no one's attention falls to the same place on the same journey. I want the moment where people have come into the room and they're talking to each other, they're looking around, they're sensing, something is vibrating in the space. But they're all in these different locations. They're not all synchronous. So as the performer or performance maker, I start to shape a landscape that has already been initiated, and different folks who have come to witness it have the time to shift. They look around, and then at some point, fifteen minutes in, they realize, Oh, something is happening here. So I like that sense in which no one begins together but, during, there's someplace

where everyone realizes they are together. So if there's this performance stage, that sense of the courtliness or a particular ritual around it, the beginning is never the beginning. But at some point, everyone gets there.

KW: That's so beautiful. When you say "gaps," though, the gaps and pauses in those spaces aren't the same as omissions. They're compositions without being negations.

OO: Oh, I like that. But negation isn't a problem either.

KW: No, not that it's a problem, but it's nice to think of pauses that aren't omissions. And within a political space, too. A lot of body politics are bound to political propaganda, and the language comes out of courtly dance.

OO: In the proscenium, there's the king seat, and everything on the stage is shaped and designed to make the king seat the optimal place for viewing. It is kind of a triangle, but it's the apex. And I really want to destroy that, the idea of one optimal viewing position. And I want to destroy the idea that everybody sees the same thing: no one will ever. It's toward deprivileging sight and making more room for shadow, and the reverberation within the shadow. That sense of order and power hierarchy, in the court, is not right. Relatedly, I'm also thinking about the prominence of the chorus in theater.

KW: The great chorus. And they turn into the parliamentary jury, that hierarchy of how the king's court decides the reproducible model or the form.

OO: Or an instantiation of some kind of particular memory. But who and what is that memory in the service of?

KW: What is the word for that? What's whitewashing before white?

OO: It's making everything clean and digestible. But it's more of an extraction. It brings questions related to storytelling: What do you want people to remember, to take away from this? Whoever has the archive, or the canon, knows very much what they want to be.

KW: Your work has given me the ability to respond. Your ability to respond and without feeling burdened by a lot of those things. Even just hearing you say, "I started before people came in." That's so meaningful. Seeing a performance that starts before the audience comes in was so useful for me and my studio. As Sylvia Wynter alludes, whiteness became a paradoxical and dissonant means of narrative construction, producing discourse of itself with only itself as referent so that there is no "before white." A shame for us, who long so much for a space before this construct of time. Bracha Ettinger calls it the *Urverdrängung* (which translates to something like the "ancient repression"), a deep-seated fantasy of before here that is a painful aspect of the object—the hanging gardens of Mycenae. We hold so many sites of mourning that aren't archaeological sites of institutional investment but foregone romantic conclusions of *colonial* storytelling. Thinking of the lecture "Shades of Intimacy" by Hortense Spillers and the etymology of the term "colony," from the Latin *colonia*, meaning "settlement, farm," from *colonus*, "settler, farmer," from *colere*, "cultivate." How are we getting behind "origins" or "starts," "vanishing points"?

OO: Because we've been starting, we've been here before. You just came. But I didn't just get here.

KW: Yes! And your performance, and the video work, has been a text that helps me understand that beginnings aren't altogether origins. Ends aren't altogether finales.

OO: It's also responsive. Not just the work, but that our bodies in the work are responding and responsive. But why does it have to be outside ourselves? We don't believe that it is within us and that we contain it within us? Or is it too narcissistic to continue to look inward? Why is it an object to project onto and not just memory?

KW: There's major conflict where the geometric body meets the figurative body. I think the virtual is this place where all of those things are knotted. We have this fourth fork of a virtual body now.

OO: But what is the space within movements and choreography and being a body moving? The space to not have to define any of that, to just reverberate with the ache in your stomach. And know that is an ache that has been felt before and will be felt after you. I don't mean to suggest there is any kind of pure form or pure movement.

KW: Bracha Ettinger and bell hooks, two of my favorite philosophers, discuss the layers of affect that form "love." For hooks, it's care, commitment, respect, knowledge, and responsibility. For Ettinger, it can be conceptual wit(h)nessing. Within Ettinger's theory of the matrixial borderspace, she uses "artworking," webs, and threads, and she spirals into the meat of Freudian repression via a metaphorical linguistic coil that is wrapped around itself, ever collapsing and expanding in the environment of the "real," not the Self, but still "I." They're both critical to how I see the space of performance and affect theory merging into social order—fetishism, internalization, primitivism, curation, origin, ritual, relationships, et cetera. There are all these spaces that are created from the tensions, provocations, discomforts, or stimulations, that both release and wind up that coil. A kind of breathing space between the Ettingerian I and non-I, and hooks's oppositional gaze.

OO: I love the sense of the matrix and multiple intersections. So maybe that's what it is, too: the multiple intersections are present all at once, nodes sparking and giving off particular charges, sending certain signals at different times. Maybe there's just pure beauty.

David Zwirner and Ebony L. Haynes wish to thank Kandis
Williams, without whom this exhibition and publication
would not have been possible. Our thanks go to Hannah
Black for her insightful text, and to Okwui Okpokwasili for
her illuminating conversation with Kandis.

For their work on the exhibition, we are grateful to Rebecca
Ashby-Colón, Claire Ball, Susan Cernek, Allison Chipak,
Cristina Covucci, Ojive DeLungéla, Coco Kim, Vida Lercari,
Thomas Ling, Julia Lukacher, Alyssa Mattocks, Kerry McFate,
Sean Morgan, Clive Murphy, Julian Phillips, Kyle Rafferty,
Robert Richburg, Gabriela Scopazzi, Janna Singer-Baefsky,
Virginia Stroh, Nora Woodin, and Lucas Zwirner.

Thank you to Andrea Hyde for the catalogue series design
and, for their work on this volume, to Claire Bidwell, Sergio
Brunelli, Luke Chase, Anna Drozda, Fabio Ferrandini,
Zeno Ferrandini, Doro Globus, Elizabeth Gordon, Jessica
Palinski, Mari Perina, Molly Stein, Jules Thomson, Chandra
Wohleber, and Joey Young.

The artist would like to thank Patrick Belaga, Stella Bouzakis,
Kelena Burwell, Natasha Diamond-Walker, Brian Echon,
Robin Ediger-Seto, Damond Garner, Michael Hernandez,
Catherine Kirk, Parent Company Films, Babak Radboy, Emily
Mei-Mei Rose, Kyejah Smith, Andy Sowers, TELFAR, Kyeree
Wright, and Charlotte Zhang.

Collections

p. 10 (top): Bundesarchiv, Bild 102-09849

p. 10 (bottom): Tate, London. Accepted by HM Government in lieu of tax with additional payment (General Funds) made with assistance from the National Lottery through the Heritage Lottery Fund, the Art Fund, the Friends of the Tate Gallery, and the Dr V.J. Daniel Bequest 1999

p. 25: Collection of Suzanne McFayden

p. 31: Private collection

pp. 43, 60: Collection of Pamela Thomas-Graham

p. 54: Private collection

p. 55: Private collection

p. 57: Private collection, Maryland

p. 59: Collection of Richard Mumby, New York

p. 64: Antonia Ax:son Johnson Family Collection

p. 66: Private collection, New York

p. 67: Collection of Alexandra Stanton and Sam Natapoff

p. 68: Ann and Mel Schaffer Family Collection

p. 69: Collection of Sukey and Mike Novogratz

pp. 71, 73, 75, 77: The Mohn Family Trust Collection

Photography

Great care has been taken to credit all images correctly. In cases of errors or omissions, please contact the publisher so that corrections can be made in future editions.

p. 8: Dance Notation Bureau, with the permission of Marie-Christine Dunham Pratt. Notator: Sandra Aberkalns

p. 10 (top): Georg Pahl

p. 10 (bottom): Tate

p. 12 (top): Martha Swope © The New York Public Library for the Performing Arts

p. 12 (bottom): © Victoria and Albert Museum, London

p. 14: © Gene Schiavone

pp. 18–19, 21, 22–23, 25, 26–27, 28–29, 31, 32–33, 35, 36–37, 39, 40–41, 43, 44–45, 46–47, 48, 49, 50, 51, 52–53, 54, 55, 56, 57, 58, 59, 60, 61, 62–63, 64, 65, 66, 67, 68, 69, 71, 73, 75, 77, 78–79: Kerry McFate

Published by David Zwirner Books
on the occasion of

Kandis Williams: A Line
52 Walker, 52 Walker Street, New York
October 28, 2021–January 8, 2022

David Zwirner Books
529 West 20th Street, 2nd Floor
New York, New York 10011
+1 212 727 2070
davidzwirnerbooks.com

Editor: Ebony L. Haynes
Project Manager: Elizabeth Gordon
Editorial Coordinator: Jessica Palinski
Copy Editor: Anna Drozda
Proofreader: Chandra Wohleber

Design: Andrea Hyde
Photography Coordinators: Rebecca Ashby-Colón, Allison Chipak, Virginia Stroh
Production: Jules Thomson, Luke Chase, Claire Bidwell
Color Separations: VeronaLibri, Verona
Printing: VeronaLibri, Verona

Typefaces: DTL Fleischmann, Genath
Paper: Magno Natural, 140 gsm

Distributed in the United States and Canada by
Simon & Schuster, Inc.
1230 Avenue of the Americas
New York, New York 10020
simonandschuster.com

Distributed outside the United States and Canada by
Thames & Hudson, Ltd.
181A High Holborn
London WC1V 7QX
thamesandhudson.com

ISBN 978-1-64423-068-8

Library of Congress Control Number: 2021925059

Printed in Italy

The *Clarion* series is an essential component of 52 Walker programming. An edition will accompany every exhibition, highlighting and expanding on the show's conceptual theses through newly commissioned texts, interviews, archival materials, and artistic interventions. The series is named in honor of the renowned author Octavia E. Butler, who was first published in the 1971 Clarion Science Fiction and Fantasy Writers' Workshop anthology.

Notes

Notes